THE
EVERYTHING ®
BARTENDER'S
BOOK

Also by Jane Parker Resnick

The Soufflé Also Rises
A Bouquet from the Kitchen
My Family History

Visit the rest of the series at
www.everything.com!

THE
EVERYTHING ®
BARTENDER'S
BOOK

Jane Parker Resnick

ADAMS MEDIA CORPORATION
Avon, Massachusetts

An Everything® Series book.
Everything® is a registered trademark of Adams Media Corporation.

Published by Adams Media Corporation
57 Littlefield Street, Avon, MA 02322. U.S.A.
www.adamsmedia.com

ISBN: 1-55850-536-9
Printed in Canada.

J

Library of Congress Cataloging-in-Publication Data
Resnick, Jane Parker
    The everything bartender's book / by Jane Parker Resnick.—1st ed.
      p.   cm.
    Includes index.
    ISBN 1-55850-536-9
    1. Bartending—Handbooks, manuals, etc. 2. Alcoholic beverages.
3. Cocktails I. Title.
    TX951.R47   1995
    641.8'74—dc20   95-34446
                                              CIP

COVER DESIGN: Barry Littmann

This book is available at quantity discounts for bulk purchases.
For information, call 1-800-872-5627.

Visit the entire Everything® Series at everything.com

CONTENTS

INTRODUCTION

Standing behind the bar is one fine place to be. As the host, it is your job to make the good times happen—and with this book you'll be prepared. If the crowd you invite includes beer drinkers as well as a more sophisticated set, you'll be able to serve them all. If your friends want to find out what Sex on the Beach is really like, you'll be ready. Above all, you can dip in and out for information, tips, ingredients, and recipes. You'll find everything from the glasses up—tools, liquors, mixers, garnishes, party ideas, and techniques. This is a textbook for fun in the one subject you won't have to force yourself to practice.

The Everything™ *Bartender's Book* begins with stocking the bar and lists all the ingredients you might want with suggestions for the basics you need to have on hand. For example, brandy might not be your personal favorite but you never know when a guest might crave a "Brandy Alexander." As long as you've got the brandy, the book has the recipe. There is also a list of the mixers you will need, along with the little accoutrements like olives and cherries, Tabasco sauce and bitters, even nutmeg for egg nog (Christmas wouldn't be the same without it).

This book gets you started with instructions that take the mystique out of making a cocktail. No great mystery here. All you need is a grasp of the difference between mixed, shaken, and blended drinks and the simple instructions on how to make them. Directions accompany every recipe. Since a bartender can't operate without the proper instruments, the tools you will need are described in detail from the corkscrew to the bar spoon.

For the sake of understanding, and sampling, the basic contents of drinks, a section is devoted to the spirits that make most cocktails possible: vodka, whiskey, scotch, bourbon, tequila, brandy, and rum. There's no bar to tend without them. Some of the greatest drinks ever invented are made with one liquor and one mixer and you'll find them all in their respective categories.

If you are going to be an everything bartender, you have to be hip to what's current and what's classic, so this book gives you the best of what's timeless—the Whiskey Sour, Tom Collins, the Sling, the Stinger, the Old-Fashioned, and other favorites with their variations and updated mutations. These aren't just drinks your grandfather would have liked. For example, a great recipe for a Bloody Mary is found in this section, a drink that has the capacity to evolve and improve with your own personal contributions. Most important, a good mixed drink does not have to include alcohol. We have dozens of recipes that taste great, look sophisticated, and allow you to have a good time, especially if you are the designated driver.

Since the only way to take bartending seriously is to think of it as serious fun, *The Everything*™ *Bartender's Book* brings you drinks grouped according to their sometimes whacky, often amusing names: Between the Sheets, Dark and Stormy, and Dead Nazi. Don't pass them up. When the right person asks, you really may want to make a terrific Soul Kiss. Whether you're looking for a funky drink to order at the bar or you intend to make it yourself, this book has it all.

The section on "Hot Stuff and Cold Concoctions" is your answer to how to make the best Piña Coladas, Daiquiris and Margaritas on the planet. It's worth buying a blender to be able to whir up a taste of tropical paradise. You'll be the bartender for all seasons, too, with recipes for hot drinks that bring a whole new dimension to the idea of warming up.

Parties could be the best territory in these pages. You'll find theme parties (like Mexican Mayhem and Hawaiian Luau), and holiday parties right through the year. You'll be the life of the party—literally—with recipes for drinks that are especially fitting and the most fun.

Sometime the best part of an evening is the beginning or the end, so this book prepares you for both with apéritifs, liqueurs and cordials, and pousse-cafés, drinks of layered liqueurs that will give you a chance to show off your bartending skills. Liqueurs are so versatile, unusual, and delicious that they create completely new drink possibilities.

We've even included a complete section on wine and champagne, starting with a brief, to-the-point education that will take you to the wine shelves of the liquor store and back to the bar with the knowledge you need to choose a wine and even mix a few outstanding cocktails. Two things you will definitely learn are how to open a champagne bottle without spraying the walls and how the bubbles got in there to begin with.

Finally, no one can stand proud behind the bar without knowing something about beer, because there are times when beer is the best. This section takes you through U-Brew to Microbrew to Beer Clubs and puts you in touch with the sources that tell you all you need to know about making, tasting, and buying beer from Alaska to Florida.

PART I
BARTENDING BEGINNINGS

Measurements Matter, Glassware, The Bartender's Tools, Stocking the Bar, Mixers, Condiments, Flourishes and Finishes, The Secret Three-Step Program for Perfect Mixed Drinks

MEASUREMENTS MATTER

Since the metric system measures the world, except in the United States, here are some equivalents to help avoid confusion. When measuring ingredients for a drink, remember that the balance is important, so for weaker or stronger drinks, adjust all of the components accordingly.

BAR MEASUREMENTS
. . . .

	Standard	Metric
1 dash	1/32 oz.	0.9 ml.
1 teaspoon	1/8 oz.	3.7 ml.
1 tablespoon	3/8 oz.	1.1 ml.
1 pony	1 oz.	29.5 ml.
1 jigger	1 1/2 oz.	44.5 ml.
1 cup	8 oz.	257 ml.

METRIC SIZES FOR SPIRITS AND WINES
. . . .

Name of Container	Standard (Fluid Ounces)	Metric
Split	6.3	187 ml.
Tenth	12.6	375 ml.
Fifth	25.3	750 ml.
Quart	33.8	1 liter
Magnum	50.7	1.5 liters
Jeroboam	101.4	3 liters

GLASSWARE: FOR THE DRINK IN HAND

There's an immediate tactile pleasure in a good drink, and it's in the glass. Fingering the stem of a cocktail glass or balancing a brandy snifter in your palm enhances the experience. To be rigid about the right glass is to be prudish in a decidedly unpuritanical pursuit, but form should not be ignored. In some cases there are essential reasons for the choice of glass. A cocktail glass is held by its stem so the hand does not warm the drink. A brandy snifter is rested in the palm, so the hand does warm the liquid and release its aroma. The narrowness of a champagne flute is not an elegant affectation, but a design to preserve the bubbles. And the frost on a beer mug is not a decoration, but a chill to hold the brew at the best taste temperature.

A *highball*, the most universally used glass, holds 8 to 12 ounces of on-the-rocks drinks like scotch and soda or gin and tonic. It's the glass of choice for everything from Planter's Punch to a Bloody Mary.

The 10- to 14-ounce *collins* glass is slimmer and taller than the highball and frosted nearly to the top. Named for the Collins family of drinks, this glass looks refreshing even when it's empty and generally holds drinks with soda or fruit that do, indeed, refresh.

The *old-fashioned* glass is for the venerable Old-Fashioned, but it's also used for most cocktails when they are requested on the rocks. Ranging from 4 to 8 ounces, the old-fashioned is the short, squat member of the glass team.

The 8- to 10-ounce *red wine* glass is balloon-shaped and the 6- to 8-ounce *white wine* is quite a bit slimmer, but there's no need to be a stickler about these dimensions. Unless perfection is a prerequisite, all-purpose wine glasses are acceptable.

Brandy snifters range considerably in size, from 5 to 25 ounces, so preference must be a guide. The brief stem allows your hand to warm the brandy and the mouth, narrower than the base, holds the aroma.

Beer is served in a *mug* or *Pilsner-style* glass to anyone except the hold outs who enjoy the brew straight from the bottle. Both the mug and the glass are usually 10 ounces. To frost a glass simply keep it in the refrigerator or immerse it in crushed ice until needed.

A *whiskey sour* glass is to the Whiskey Sour what an old-fashioned glass is to the Old-Fashioned: traditional. At 4 to 6 ounces, it fits the ingredients of its namesake perfectly, with or without ice. Although the stem is shorter than that of a cocktail glass, it can still be held neatly between the fingers so the drink is kept from the heat of your hands.

The *cocktail* glass is the symbol of drinking establishments throughout the world. Designed like an upside down Chinese straw hat on a stem, it holds the ingredients over a wide surface so they are least likely to separate. The stem gives you a good grip without putting your hand to the glass and warming the drink.

The *Irish coffee* mug is a soul-warming container for all hot drinks. At 8 to 10 ounces, it offers enough volume for the right proportions of spirits and non-alcoholic ingredients and its handle allows you to hold the glass while the drink is still properly hot.

The *parfait*, while certainly not a bar essential, is festive for blended concoctions. Its purpose is more decorative than practical, and it adds to the enjoyment of drinks that are fun to begin with.

A 3- to 4-ounce *sherry* glass holds many of the before and after dinner drinks, such as sherry, port, and various apéritifs. These are, by definition, small drinks, and the size of the sherry glass is right for the portion.

A 1-ounce liqueur glass is also known as a *cordial* glass or a *"pony."* Pour a pousse-café in the pony for the strangest combination behind the bar.

The 1- or 2-ounce *shot* glass does double duty as a measurer and a serving glass.

Champagne is served appropriately in either a 4- to 6-ounce stemmed, *wide-mouthed* glass or a 7- to 10-ounce *flute*, and the choice does make a difference. The open surface of the wide-mouthed glass allows the carbonation to escape, while the narrow flute works to preserve the bubbles.

THE BARTENDER'S TOOLS

There's always a buzz of anticipation when a host asks, "What would you like to drink?" But nothing punctures this suave statement like the lack of a bottle opener. Equipment matters. A surgeon wouldn't dash into the kitchen for a knife. A bartender shouldn't have to scramble through the gadget drawer for a corkscrew. Of course, space matters too. If a corner of the kitchen is the bar, try to arrange all equipment together with small utensils in a basket so they will be handy. Keeping measuring spoons there, for example, eliminates the possibility of their being buried in baking paraphernalia when needed. Here is a list of essential utensils. Don't scrimp. Without tools, even the simplest drink becomes complicated. A naked bar makes for a bumbling bartender.

Can and bottle openers. Old-fashioned bottle openers that also puncture cans are still a bar staple. Puncturing a can of fruit juice or coconut cream is the most functional way to pour at the bar.

Corkscrew. The most professional corkscrew is the "waiter's" version, a three-in-one gadget that opens wine, bottles, and cans. Here's how

to use it to open a wine bottle: Remove the foil around the top of the cork. Insert the screw into the center of the cork and twist until it's nearly all the way into the cork. Pull the cork straight out of the bottle—gently. A wing-type corkscrew is another choice that is easy to use.

Shaker set. For shaken drinks, the shaker set is two flat bottomed cones that fit inside each other. Stainless steel and glass is the right combination.

Strainer. The strainer is a metal and wire arrangement that fits over the shaker so chilled drinks can be poured into a glass without the ice cubes. Essential.

Ice bucket and tongs are to keep ice on hand and frozen longer.

Barspoon. The giraffe of spoons, the barspoon's neck is extra long for mixing drinks, and twisted for making pousse-cafés.

Fruit juice extractor or citrus reamer. These are fancy names for a hands-on juicer. Fresh juice is a small effort that goes a long way.

Measuring spoons and 1 cup measuring cup.

Paring knife. Used for fruit. A small *cutting board* is a good partner to the knife.

Mixing glass. This glass is the key to stirred drinks and very important. The glass part of a shaker set is often used.

Pitcher. Fruit juice, Bloody Mary mix, water, there's always something that a pitcher can be used for behind the bar.

Jigger/Pony. This utensil measures 1 ½ ounces on the jigger side and 1 ounce on the pony side—a more accurate measuring technique than eye-balling.

Muddler. This is a mortar and pestle affair, wood or ceramic, to crush mint and muddle sugar and fruit. Improvisation is allowed here; often the back of a wooden spoon will do. Muddlers are most likely to be available in stores that specialize in kitchen equipment.

Blender. A bar without a blender is a bar without frozen daiquiris. The heavier the motor, the better for crushing ice.

Champagne stopper. The spring in this stopper will help to keep the bubbles in the bottle.

Straws are served with some cocktails and blended drinks.

Swizzle sticks are used for mixing when a shared spoon is not an option.

Finally, no bar should be without *napkins.*

STOCKING THE BAR

Marines, boy scouts, and bartenders should always be prepared. Stocking a bar should be a matter of personal taste, lifestyle, and finances. But unless having a drink is always going to be a solitary pleasure, the person behind the bar should be prepared for guests. How prepared is up to you. If Uncle Michael, who always visits at Christmas, only smiles with a glass of Irish whiskey in his hand, buy one bottle. If cognac inspires camaraderie among your friends, make the investment. If beer does the trick, stick to what works. Here are two suggested lists, one for a basic home bar and another that goes beyond basic to *complete.*

LIQUORS

Basic Bar	*Add for Complete Bar*
Bourbon	Canadian Whiskey
Brandy and Cognac	Dark Rum
Gin	Citrus-flavored Vodka
Rum	Russian Vodka
Scotch	Gold Tequila
Tequila	Grappa
Vodka	Single Malt Scotch
Whiskey (Irish)	Armagnac
Blended whiskey or rye	

WINE AND FORTIFIED WINES

Basic Bar	*Add for Complete Bar*
Red, dry (Cabernet Sauvignon)	Champagne, Brut
White, dry (Chardonnay, refrigerated)	Rosé
Vermouth, sweet and dry	Port, tawny and ruby
Sherry, dry	Dubonnet, blanc and rouge
	Campari
	Sherry, fino and cream
	Lillet
	Madeira

BEER

Basic Bar	Add for Complete Bar
Lager	Ale
Lite	Porter

LIQUERS AND OTHER DRINKS

Basic Bar	Add for Complete Bar
Applejack or Calvados	B & B
Amaretto	Chambord
Anisette	Drambuie
Cointreau or Triple Sec	Fruit-flavored brandies, cherry and apricot
Crème de Banane	Galliano
Crème de Cacao, light and dark	Schnapps, peach and peppermint
Crème de Menthe, white and green	Chartreuse, green and yellow
Crème de Noyaux	Frangelico
Crème de Cassis	Kirschwasser
Grand Marnier	Jagermeister
Pernod	Maraschino
Amer Picon	Midori
Benedictine	Tuaca
Kahlúa	Vandermint
Sambuca, white	Irish Mist
Bailey's Irish Cream	Strega
Curaçao, white and blue	Tia Maria
Sloe Gin	Frambois
Southern Comfort	Forbidden Fruit

MIXERS

Mixers provide the flavor and balance that, combined with liquor, give a drink its distinctive taste. Mixers range from plain water to club soda to tonic, from flavored sodas (like cola and lemon and lime) to fruit juices (orange, pineapple, cranberry, grapefruit, and tomato), and others. When it comes to mixers, fresher is better. Fresh lemon and lime juices are the primary mixers, even though they are most often added in one ounce portions. Their acid zing is a catalyst for the successful mingling of flavors. A convenient way to use fresh juice is a small hand or electric citrus reamer. When buying juices, look for those sweetened naturally, in bottles, not cans. In the dairy case, choose juice labeled "not from concentrate." At first, follow the recipes for the proportions of alcohol and mixers and then experiment, improvise, substitute. There really are no rules, just taste tests, so have fun mixing up what you like best.

Sugar is a powerful partner in many drinks, but its presence is behind the scenes, never tasted distinctly, and never, never felt as granules. Unless granulated sugar is specified, confectioner's sugar, referred to in this book as fine sugar, should always be used. Some bartenders go a step further and prepare a "simple syrup" of sugar and water to use instead of dry sugar. To make a simple syrup, heat 2 cups of water in a saucepan and slowly add 1 pound of granulated sugar until it is completely dissolved. The syrup can be stored in a bottle in a cool place.

A word about prepared drink mixes. Well, maybe not. Uniform praise or condemnation is impossible because the quality of products varies. Also, with this book's bias for "fresher is better," it is difficult to be objective. You can buy prepared mixes for Collinses, Daiquiris, Margaritas, and, of course, Bloody Marys, among others. They come in bottled and powdered form, some are excellent and some are not. So let the bartender beware and be the judge. "Sour" mixes, which contain lemon juice, sugar, and some egg white, are a special case. Whenever a recipe in this book calls for sugar and the juice of one half lemon, sour mix can be substituted in the amount indicated on the product's label.

While the sound of "bitters" is not appealing, the little, elaborately papered bottles are, and so are their ingredients, a witch's brew of roots and barks, berries and herbs. Bitters add a kick of flavor to the mixed drinks they accompany, always in small amounts, dashes, to be approximately exact. The most common type of bitters is Angostura, made in Trinidad. Two that are sometimes used are Peychaud's, from New Orleans, and Orange Bitters, an English product that would make anyone who enjoys a sweet orange cry. Bitters do have an alcohol content and should not be served to anyone who abstains totally. Tasting them plain is not recommended either.

The following is a list of mixers for a basic and more complete home bar.

MIXERS
• •

Basic Bar	*Add for Complete Bar*
Angostura Bitters	Simple syrup
Club Soda	Pineapple juice
Tonic Water	Cranberry juice
Cola	Coconut Cream
Diet Cola and other diet	Ginger beer
sodas	Grapefruit juice
Ginger Ale	Peach nectar
Lemon and lime soda	Passion Fruit juice
Orange juice	Raspberry syrup
Tomato juice	Clamato juice
Grenadine	Frozen lemonade
Rose's lime juice	Frozen limeade
(sweetened, not to be	Frozen raspberry juice
substituted for lime juice)	Frozen tropical juice
Lemons for fresh lemon juice	Beef bouillon
Limes for fresh lime juice	Coffee
Milk	Peychaud's Bitters
Light cream	Orange Bitters
Tabasco sauce	
Worcestershire sauce	
Bottled water	

CONDIMENTS: THE LITTLE THINGS IN LIFE

Salt and pepper, cinnamon and nutmeg, sugar and spice are all needed at the bar. Drinks are a delicate balance of ingredients, a microcosm of flavors. When the drink that is being created only totals three to eight ounces, every dash, splash, and fraction of a teaspoon counts. Condiments are like the little things in life— they make all the difference. Stocking the bar with them is not an exaggerated effort, but as basic as buying the liquor. For some people, a Martini does not exist without an olive, a Margarita is naked without its salt. A Gibson is, in fact, defined by its cocktail onion. A collection of condiments is dependent on personal needs. The accompanying list includes items like celery stalks and horseradish for Bloody Marys that you cannot keep at the bar waiting, but must be available when the drinks are made. However, coarse salt for Margaritas can be ready at any time.

CONDIMENTS
. . . .

Basic Bar	*Add for Complete Bar*
Coarse salt	Cinnamon sticks
Fine sugar	Celery sticks
Pepper	Bananas
Horseradish	Fresh mint
Cocktail onions	Ground cloves
Cocktail olives	Orgeat (almond) syrup
Maraschino cherries	Pineapple
Cinnamon	Oranges
Nutmeg	Eggs (refrigerated)

FLOURISHES AND FINISHES

There is enough muddling in life as it is—why learn more behind the bar? Because "muddling" takes on a new meaning at the bar, along with "twist" and "chill." Every effort has its particular skills, peculiar jargon, and specialized gadgets. Bartending is no different—just more fun.

MAKING A MUDDLE
· · · · · · · · · · · · · · · · ·

Muddling was not invented by Southerners; the Mint Julep just makes it seem that way. Muddling is simply mashing, usually herbs and sugar or fruit and sugar, so that the flavors will be fully released and blend together beautifully.

A muddler, a small bowl and masher, facilitates the task, but the back of a spoon pressed into the bottom of a drink's glass will do.

DOING THE TWIST
· · · · · · · · · · · · · · · · ·

The lemon twist is not an art form, but it's more than just paring off an edge of rind. To create artful twists, cut off both ends of the lemon so the fruit shows. Make a slit in the fruit from end to end. Squeeze a bar spoon beneath the skin and scoop out the fruit. Cut the peel into quarter-inch strips.

The proper way to add a twist is to twist the peel, colored side down, over the drink, so the oils will release. Then, rub the colored side around the rim and drop the twist into the drink.

CUTTING THE WEDGE
· · · · · · · · · · · · · · · · ·

The tang of a lime wedge and the flavor of its juice are never superfluous. To cut the essential wedge, slice a lime in half through the center and cut each half into four wedges.

When serving, squeeze the juice into the drink, rub the fruit side around the rim of the glass, and drop the lime in the liquor.

A CHILLING IDEA
· · · · · · · · · · · · · · · · · ·

Pouring a cold drink into a warm glass is not a crime, but it should be. It robs the drink of its chill and the pleasure of its proper temperature. Chilling glasses is not hard, of course, just difficult to remember. If refrigerator or freezer space allows, squeeze the glasses in along with the ice cream. If not, fill a glass with ice just before serving, stir it a bit, and discard the ice.

THE SECRET THREE-STEP PROGRAM FOR PERFECT MIXED DRINKS

There are three basic types of mixed drinks: highballs, stirred cocktails, and shaken cocktails. Grasp these and you'll stand proud behind the bar with confidence and very little fancy footwork. With the briefest experience, the techniques become automatic, and the satisfaction of mixing a good drink for friends is almost as good as having one.

The Highball. Pouring a tall glass of orange juice in the morning is about as complicated as making a highball. Think Screwdriver. Fill a highball glass about two-thirds with ice. Pour in a 1½-ounce jigger of vodka, or whatever measure the moment calls for. Pour orange juice to fill. Stir. That's it. If a drink, like Rum and Coke, calls for a carbonated mixer, don't stir or stir very gently, so as not to disrupt the bubbles. Garnish if called for by the recipe.

The Stirred Cocktail. The simple act of stirring transforms a drink into more than the sum of its parts. A stirred drink can be served "straight up," without ice, in a cocktail glass, or "on the rocks," over ice, in an old-fashioned glass. It can even be made right in the rocks

1

2

glass, but the flourish and finish of classic
stirring is worth the effort. For an example, take
the Manhattan.

Begin by nearly filling a shaker glass with
ice. Pour in the ingredient of the smallest
amount, three-quarters of an ounce of sweet
vermouth. Add 2 ounces of blended whiskey or
3 ounces for a stronger version. Stir—really
stir—with the straight end of a bar spoon.
What you are doing is introducing the liquids to
the ice, and chilling them. Then hold a strainer
over the glass and pour into a cocktail glass. Or
pour over new ice into a rocks glass. Garnish
with a cherry.

The Shaken Cocktail. Shaking will not
"bruise" the gin in a Martini, as James Bond
once warned, nor does it require athletic
training. Dexterity is only necessary to hold the
two parts of the shaker together so the drink
doesn't end up on the floor. Anybody can do
that. Shaking is appropriate for drinks with fruit
juices, sugar, eggs, and cream. For example, try
a Brandy Alexander.

Begin by nearly filling a shaker glass with
ice. Pour in 1 ounce of crème de cacao, 1 ounce
of cream, and then 1$\frac{1}{2}$ ounces of brandy.
Actual shaking depends on the type of shaker

3

used. With a glass and stainless steel shaker, cover the glass with the steel shell. Hold firmly with one hand on each container and push to seal them tightly. Shake up and down, still holding with two hands. Then hold the glass part upright and tap the metal top with the heel of your hand to loosen it. Turn over so the contents drain into the metal half. Place a strainer over the top, to hold the ice, and pour into a cocktail glass. Dust with nutmeg.

PART II
LIQUORS—STRAIGHT UP OR MIXED

Vodka, Whiskey, Scotch, Bourbon, Tequila, Brandy, Rum

VODKA: THE SPIRITED NEUTRAL

The measures of a great vodka are all negative superlatives: tasteless, odorless, and colorless. Vodka is the profound silent partner to all with which it mixes. In the 1930s, the Smirnoff family brought vodka to America from Russia where it had been distilled primarily from potatoes and acquired its diminutive, affectionate name, "dear little water." Today vodka is produced mostly from grains in a three-step process including charcoal filtering that makes it very pure and very potent. Its proof ranges from 80 to 100, which makes the liquor neither "dear" nor "little." Because vodka is chameleon-like in taking on the tastes of what surrounds it, flavored versions have come into vogue, notably pepper and citrus. Nonetheless, vodka, the spirited spirit, has its own, intense character.

Vodka on the Rocks

2 oz.   vodka
          lemon twist

Place a few ice cubes in an old-fashioned glass and add vodka. Garnish with a lemon twist.

Vodka and Tonic

2 oz.   vodka
          tonic water

Fill a highball glass with ice. Pour vodka. Top with tonic. Stir. Garnish with a lemon wedge.

Godmother

2 oz.   vodka
1 oz.   Amaretto

Pour into old-fashioned glass over ice. Stir.

Silverado

1½ oz.   vodka
1½ oz.   Campari
1 oz.   orange juice

Combine ingredients in an old-fashioned glass over ice. Stir.

Cape Cod

1½ oz.   vodka
5 oz.   cranberry juice

Pour into a highball glass over ice. Stir. Serve with a wedge of lime.

Mudslide

1 oz.   vodka
1 oz.   Irish cream liqueur
1 oz.   coffee brandy

Pour ingredients into a mixing glass nearly filled with ice. Stir well. Strain into a cocktail glass.

Bull Shot

1½ oz.   vodka
4 oz.   chilled beef bouillon
dash   Worcestershire sauce
          salt and pepper

Combine ingredients in a shaker half filled with ice. Shake well. Strain into a highball glass over ice.

Harvey Wallbanger

1½ oz.   vodka
4 oz.   orange juice
1 oz.   Galliano

Pour vodka and orange juice into a collins glass over ice. Stir. Float Galliano on top.

Blue Lagoon

1 oz.   vodka
1 oz.   blue Curaçao
          lemonade

Pour vodka and Curaçao into a highball glass over ice. Stir. Fill with lemonade.

Sunny Lagoon
(Non-alcoholic)

2 oz.	lemon juice or juice of 1 lemon
2 tsp.	granulated sugar
5 oz.	chilled water

Dissolve the sugar in the lemon juice in a collins glass. Stir well. Add ice. Add water. Garnish with lemon.

Aqueduct

1½ oz.	vodka
1 tsp.	Curaçao
1 tsp.	apricot brandy
1 Tbs.	lime juice

Combine ingredients in a shaker half filled with ice. Shake well. Strain into a cocktail glass. Serve with a lemon twist.

Cosmopolitan

1 oz.	citrus-flavored vodka
½ oz.	Cointreau
½ oz.	cranberry juice
¼ oz.	lime juice

Combine ingredients in a shaker half filled with ice. Shake well. Strain into a cocktail glass.

Citronella Cooler

1 oz.	lemon vodka
2 oz.	lemonade
2 oz.	cranberry juice
splash	lime juice

Pour over ice into a highball or collins glass. Garnish with a lime wedge.

Citronella Fella
(Non-alcoholic)

2 oz.	lemonade
2 oz.	limeade
2 oz.	cranberry juice
splash	club soda

Pour over ice into a highball or collins glass. Garnish with a lime wedge.

Seabreeze

1½ oz.	vodka
3 oz.	cranberry juice
2 oz.	grapefruit juice

Pour into a highball glass over ice. Garnish with a lime wedge.

Soft Breeze
(Non-alcoholic)

3 oz.	cranberry juice
3 oz.	grapefruit juice
splash	lime juice

Pour into a highball glass over ice. Garnish with a lime wedge.

Liquors—Straight Up or Mixed *31*

Fuzzy Navel

1 oz. vodka
1 oz. peach-flavored
       brandy
4 oz. orange juice

Pour into a highball glass over ice.
Stir well.

Unfuzzy Navel
(Non-alcoholic)

3 oz. peach nectar
3 oz. orange juice
1 tsp. lemon juice
dash   grenadine

Combine ingredients in a shaker half
filled with ice. Shake well. Strain into a
red wine glass. Garnish with a fruit slice.

Orange Crush Shooter

¾ oz. vodka
¾ oz. Triple Sec
splash club soda

Combine ingredients in a mixing
glass nearly filled with ice. Stir.
Strain into a shot glass.

Lemon Drop Shooter

1½ oz vodka
       sugar
       lemon wedge

Pour chilled vodka into a shot glass.
Coat lemon with sugar. To drink: take
shot, suck lemon.

Galactic Ale Shooter

1 oz. vodka
1 oz. blue Curaçao
½ oz. crème de cassis
splash lime juice

Combine ingredients in a shaker half
filled with ice. Shake well. Strain into
a shot glass.

Windex Shooter

¾ oz. vodka
¾ oz. blue Curaçao

Combine ingredients in a mixing
glass nearly filled with ice. Stir.
Strain into a shot glass.

Jello Shots

Jello shots are a contemporary creation, a textured drink. Think jiggly
or slushy or syrupy. Imagine the slide
of a semi-solid in your mouth. Then
make your personal jello shots.
Nothing else comes close. Luckily.

6 oz. vodka
6 oz. water
3 oz. Jello gelatin,
       any flavor

Combine vodka and water in a
saucepan and bring to a boil. Stir in
Jello. Let set in the refrigerator.
Experiment to choose the degree to
which you prefer the jello to set. The
longer in the fridge, the firmer it will be.

WHISKEY ALL WAYS

Whiskey is multifaceted. It is bourbon or rye, straight (from a single grain) or blended (a combination of one or more straight whiskeys and neutral grain spirits). It is made in America, Canada, Ireland, and Scotland (where it is quite simply Scotch). The "e" in whiskey appears on American and Irish brands; Canada and Scotland spell it "whisky." All straight whiskeys must have 51 percent of a single ingredient. Therefore, rye is 51 percent rye; bourbon, 51 percent corn; malt whiskey (Scotch), 51 percent barley. Straight corn whiskey is 80 percent corn. *And* there is Tennessee whiskey, which must be made in that state to carry the name. The proportion of grains and the different aging processes are responsible for each whiskey's quite individual flavor. But the technical side of this liquor never interferes with its pleasures. Whiskey is wonderful with or without an "e."

Whiskey Highball

2 oz.   blended whiskey
         club soda

Pour liquor into a highball glass nearly filled with ice cubes. Top with soda. Garnish with a lemon twist.

Seven & Seven

2 oz.   Seagram's 7
5 oz.   7-Up

Pour liquor into a highball glass nearly filled with ice cubes. Top with soda. Garnish with a lemon twist.

Algonquin

1½ oz.   rye whiskey
1 oz.   dry vermouth
1 oz.   pineapple juice

Combine all ingredients in a shaker nearly filled with ice. Shake. Strain into a cocktail glass.

Rye and Ginger

2 oz.   rye whiskey
         ginger ale
         lemon twist

Fill a highball glass with ice. Pour whiskey. Fill with ginger ale. Add a twist of lemon and stir.

Black Hawk

1½ oz.   blended whiskey
1½ oz.   sloe gin

Combine ingredients in a mixing glass half filled with ice. Stir. Strain into a cocktail glass. Serve with a cherry.

Ward 8

1½ oz.   rye whiskey
½ oz.   orange juice
½ oz.   lemon juice
dash   grenadine

Combine ingredients in a shaker half filled with ice. Shake well. Strain into a cocktail glass.

T.N.T.

1½ oz.   blended whiskey
1 oz.   Anisette

Combine ingredients in a shaker half filled with ice. Shake well. Strain into a cocktail glass.

Blarney Stone

2 oz.	Irish whiskey
½ tsp.	Anisette
½ tsp.	Cointreau
½ tsp.	Maraschino
dash	bitters

Combine ingredients in a shaker half filled with ice. Shake well. Strain into a cocktail glass. Add an olive.

Canadian Cocktail

1½ oz.	Canadian whisky
½ oz.	Cointreau
1 tsp.	fine sugar
dash	bitters

Combine ingredients in a shaker half filled with ice. Shake well. Strain into a cocktail glass.

Lady's Cocktail

1½ oz.	blended whiskey
½ tsp.	Anisette
dash	bitters

Pour ingredients into a mixing glass nearly filled with ice. Stir. Strain into a cocktail glass.

California Lemonade

2 oz.	blended whiskey
1 Tbs.	fine sugar
1 oz.	lemon juice or juice of ½ lemon
1 oz.	lime juice or juice of ½ lime
	club soda

Pour all ingredients except club soda into a shaker half filled with ice. Shake well. Pour into a highball or collins glass with ice. Add club soda and stir. Garnish with fruit slice and cherry.

California Lite (Non-alcoholic)

3 oz.	lemonade
3 oz.	limeade
	club soda

Pour lemonade and limeade into a highball glass over ice. Stir. Add soda to fill. Stir gently. Garnish with fruit and a cherry.

Spy Catcher Shooter

| 1 oz. | Canadian whisky |
| ½ oz. | Sambuca |

Combine ingredients in a mixing glass half filled with ice. Stir. Strain ingredients into a shot glass.

Canadian Cherry

2 oz.	Canadian whisky
1/2 oz.	cherry-flavored brandy
1 tsp.	lemon juice
2 tsp.	orange juice

Combine all ingredients in a shaker nearly filled with ice. Shake well. Pour into an old-fashioned glass over ice cubes. Garnish with a cherry.

Canadian Cherry (Non-alcoholic)

2 oz.	cherry soda
1 oz.	orange juice
1 tsp.	lemon juice

Pour into an old-fashioned glass over ice cubes. Stir well. Garnish with a cherry.

T-Bird

1 1/2 oz.	Canadian whisky
1/2 oz.	Amaretto
2 oz.	pineapple juice
1 oz.	orange juice

Combine all ingredients in a shaker nearly filled with ice. Shake well. Pour into a highball glass over ice cubes. Garnish with a fruit slice and cherry. Serve with a straw.

Sweet Bird (Non-alcoholic)

2 oz.	pineapple juice
2 oz.	orange juice
1 oz.	lemonade
1 Tbs.	crushed pineapple

Spoon crushed pineapple into a highball glass. Add lemonade and stir well. Add ice. Add juices and stir. Garnish with a fruit slice and cherry.

SOPHISTICATED SCOTCH

For those who know little of Scotland but savor its whisky, it is the land of kilts, the Loch Ness monster, and Scotch—and that's all they care to know. Actually, there is a great deal to know about Scotch itself and the different brands that are so individual. Briefly, there are two basic types, single malt and blended. The single malt is made from a single distillation of malted barley, while the blended contains a combination of single malts and grain whiskies. The distinct taste differences in all Scotches are caused by the air quality, peat bogs, and water where the liquor is made, a fact that should make ardent environmentalists out of all Scotch drinkers. There are eight regions of single malt producers in Scotland and the product of each is unique. Admirers of single malts usually are devotees of a particular brand. Enthusiasts of a blended label maintain that the art is in the blending. But few would deny the supremacy of Scotch in the domain of whisky.

Scotch on the Rocks

2 oz.   scotch

Pour scotch into an old-fashioned glass over ice.

Balmoral

1½ oz.	scotch
½ oz.	sweet vermouth
½ oz.	dry vermouth
2 dashes	bitters

Combine all ingredients in a mixing glass half filled with ice. Stir. Strain into a cocktail glass.

Godfather

| 1½ oz. | scotch |
| ¾ oz. | Amaretto |

Pour scotch and Amaretto into an old-fashioned glass over ice.

Scotch Mist

2 oz.   scotch
           crushed ice

Fill an old-fashioned glass with ice. Pour in scotch and serve with a straw.

Rusty Nail

| 2 oz. | scotch |
| 1 oz. | Drambuie |

Pour scotch and Drambuie into an old-fashioned glass filled with ice cubes. Stir.

Black Watch

1½ oz.	scotch
1 oz.	coffee brandy
splash	soda

Pour ingredients into a mixing glass nearly filled with ice. Stir. Strain into a cocktail glass.

Loch Lomond

1 oz.	scotch
1 oz.	blue Curaçao
½ oz.	peach-flavored brandy
3 oz.	grapefruit juice
½ oz.	lemon juice
	crushed ice

Pour all ingredients into a shaker half filled with ice. Shake well. Strain into a collins or parfait glass filled with crushed ice. Garnish with a fruit slice.

Lomond Fruit Crush (Non-alcoholic)

¼ cup	blueberries, fresh or frozen
1 oz.	peach nectar
2 oz.	grapefruit juice
½ oz.	lemon juice

Combine ingredients in a blender with ice. Blend well. Pour into a collins or parfait glass. Garnish with fruit. Serve with a straw.

Bobby Burns

1½ oz.	scotch
1½ oz.	sweet vermouth
1 tsp.	Benedictine

Pour ingredients into a mixing glass nearly filled with ice. Stir. Strain into a cocktail glass.

Perfect Rob Roy

2 oz.	scotch
1 tsp.	sweet vermouth
1 tsp.	dry vermouth

Pour ingredients into a mixing glass nearly filled with ice. Stir. Strain into a cocktail glass. Garnish with a lemon twist.

Scotch Holiday Sour

1½ oz.	scotch
1 oz.	cherry brandy
½ oz.	sweet vermouth
1 oz.	lemon juice or juice of ½ lemon

Combine ingredients in a shaker half filled with ice. Shake well. Strain into an old-fashioned glass over ice.

Heather Blush

1 oz.	scotch
1 oz.	crème de cassis
3 oz.	chilled sparkling wine

Pour scotch and crème de cassis into a champagne glass. Fill with sparkling wine.

Blushing Heather (Non-alcoholic)

1 oz.	raspberry syrup
3 oz.	sparkling white grape juice
splash	lemon juice

Pour raspberry syrup and lemon juice into a champagne glass. Stir. Fill with sparkling grape juice.

Blinder

2 oz.	scotch
5 oz.	grapefruit juice
1 tsp.	grenadine

Pour scotch and grapefruit juice into an ice-filled highball glass. Add grenadine and stir slightly.

Eyeful
(Non-alcoholic)

4 oz.	pink grapefruit juice
1 oz.	tonic water
½ oz.	grenadine
1 tsp.	fine sugar

Combine ingredients in a shaker half filled with ice. Shake well. Strain into a highball glass over ice.

Modern Cocktail

1½ oz.	scotch
1 tsp.	dark rum
½ tsp.	Anisette
½ tsp.	lemon juice
2 dashes	orange bitters

Pour all ingredients into a shaker half filled with ice. Shake well. Strain into a cocktail glass.

Remsen Cooler

2 oz.	scotch
½ tsp.	fine sugar
4 oz.	club soda
	lemon twist

Dissolve sugar in a splash of club soda in a collins or highball glass. Add ice. Pour scotch. Stir. Add club soda. Add a lemon twist.

Affinity

2 oz.	scotch
½ oz.	sweet vermouth
½ oz.	dry vermouth
3 dashes	bitters

Combine all ingredients in a shaker nearly filled with ice. Shake. Strain into a cocktail glass.

ALL-AMERICAN BOURBON

It's no surprise that the Mint Julep and bourbon have the same home territory, Bourbon County, Kentucky. Bourbon whiskey, born in the late 1700s, is America's original native brew. Like most liquors, its ingredients are humble—corn and wood. But bourbon's distinctive flavor emerges from its 51 percent corn mash and the charred oak barrels in which the liquor ages. A "mash," the source of all whiskies and beers, is milled cereal cooked in water. The quality of that water is all-important. Eighty percent of the world's bourbon is produced in America because the clear limestone spring water of the Kentucky hills makes this bourbon the best.

The amber color, sweetness, and amount of rye, wheat, or barley added to the mash characterize the different brands of bourbon. No two have exactly the same recipe. Straying most from the classic is a blend of peach liqueur and bourbon known as Southern Comfort. It's a wonderful name, but probably not a drink the originators of bourbon would have liked. They called their liquor whiskey and, no doubt, they liked it straight.

Bourbon on the Rocks

2 oz.   bourbon

Pour bourbon into an old-fashioned glass nearly filled with ice. Stir

Bourbon and Branch

This drink is the upscale version of bourbon and water, using mineral water as the "branch."

2 oz.   bourbon
4 oz.   mineral water

Pour bourbon and water into an old-fashioned glass nearly filled with ice. Stir. Add a twist of lemon if desired.

Kentucky Colonel or Kentucky B & B

1½ oz.   bourbon
½ oz.   Benedictine

Combine ingredients in a mixing glass half filled with ice. Stir. Strain into a cocktail glass. Serve with a lemon twist.

Bourbon Highball

2 oz.   bourbon
          ginger ale or
          club soda

Pour bourbon and soda into a highball glass nearly filled with ice. Serve with a twist of lemon.

J. R.'s Godfather

2 oz.   bourbon
½ oz.   Amaretto

Pour bourbon and Amaretto into an old-fashioned glass nearly filled with ice. Stir well.

Bull and Bear

2 oz.   bourbon
1 oz.   orange Curaçao
1 Tbs.   grenadine
1 oz.   lime juice or
          juice of ½ lime

Combine ingredients in a shaker half filled with ice. Shake well. Strain into a cocktail glass. Garnish with a cherry.

Nevins

2 oz.	bourbon
1/2 oz.	apricot brandy
1/2 oz.	grapefruit juice
1 tsp.	lemon juice
dash	bitters

Combine all ingredients in a shaker half filled with ice cubes. Shake well. Strain into a cocktail glass.

Gentleman's Cocktail

2 oz.	bourbon
1/2 oz.	crème de menthe
1/2 oz.	brandy
4 oz.	club soda

Pour liquors into a highball glass nearly filled with ice. Add club soda. Garnish with a lemon twist.

Southern Lady

2 oz.	bourbon
1 oz.	Southern Comfort
1 oz.	Amaretto
3 oz.	pineapple juice
2 oz.	lemon and lime soda

Combine the bourbon, Southern Comfort, Amaretto, and pineapple juice in a shaker half filled with ice. Shake. Strain into a collins or parfait glass. Add soda. Garnish with fruit and a cherry.

Southern Sister (Non-alcoholic)

1/4 cup	crushed pineapple
3 oz.	pineapple juice
3 oz.	club soda

Combine pineapple and juice in a blender without ice. Blend well. Pour into a collins glass. Add ice. Add soda and stir. Garnish with fruit.

Bourbon Satin

1½ oz.	bourbon
1 oz.	white crème de menthe
1 oz.	light cream

Combine ingredients in a shaker half filled with ice. Shake well. Strain into a cocktail glass.

Rocky Mountain Shooter

1 oz.	Southern Comfort
1 oz.	Amaretto
½ oz.	lime juice

Combine ingredients in a shaker half filled with ice. Shake well. Strain into a shot glass.

Alabama Slammer Shooter

½ oz.	Southern Comfort
1 oz.	Amaretto
½ oz.	Sloe Gin
splash	lemon juice

Stir ingredients in a mixing glass half filled with ice. Strain into a shot glass. Add lemon juice.

TEQUILA: MEXICAN BEAUTY

Legend has it that the Aztec ruler, Montezuma, welcomed the Spanish explorer Cortez with a drink from the agave plant. Poor man. The ungrateful Cortez became his conqueror, but we can be grateful that the drink became tequila. With its distinctive dry taste, tequila is the basis for marvelous drinks, not the least of which is the Margarita. This liquor is produced only in Mexico, from the blue agave or century plant, found in specific regions of the country. Colorless tequila is not aged, but the gold version is usually two to four years old. Anejo is tequila aged in oak barrels where it acquires its mellow color of gold.

Government regulation is also the difference between mescal and tequila. Basically, mescal has no controls and can be produced anywhere in Mexico, from agaves that are not necessarily blue. And, then there's the worm. Mescal, not tequila, is the Mexican brew with a worm in the bottle.

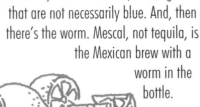

Tequila Straight

1½ oz.   tequila
pinch   salt
lemon wedge

Pour tequila into a shot glass. To drink: sprinkle salt on the back of your left hand; hold glass in the left hand and the lemon wedge in the right. Lick salt, drink tequila, suck lemon. Olé!

Mexicola or Claudio's Tequila

2 oz.   tequila
cola
lime wedge

Pour tequila into a highball glass over ice. Add cola to fill. Stir. Squeeze a lime wedge as garnish.

Spanish Moss

1 oz.   tequila
1 oz.   coffee liqueur
1 oz.   crème de menthe

Combine ingredients in a mixing glass half filled with ice. Stir. Strain into an old-fashioned glass over ice.

La Bomba

1½ oz.   tequila
½ oz.   Cointreau
1½ oz.   pineapple juice
1½ oz.   orange juice
splash   grenadine

Combine ingredients in a shaker nearly filled with ice. Shake well. Strain into a cocktail glass.

La Boom (Non-alcoholic)

4 oz.   orange juice
4 oz.   pineapple juice
splash   grenadine
squeeze   lime
squeeze   lemon

Combine ingredients in a shaker half filled with ice. Shake well. Strain into a collins glass. Garnish with fruit. Serve with a straw.

Silk Stockings

1½ oz.   tequila
1 oz.   crème de cacao
1 oz.   cream
dash   grenadine

Combine ingredients in a shaker nearly filled with ice. Shake well. Strain into a cocktail glass.

Shady Lady

1 oz.   tequila
1 oz.   Midori
4 oz.   grapefruit juice

Combine ingredients in a mixing glass half filled with ice. Stir. Strain into a highball glass over ice. Garnish with fruit and a cherry.

Proper Lady
(Non-alcoholic)

¼ cup   melon, cut up
5 oz.   grapefruit juice
1 tsp. lemon juice

Combine melon, lemon juice, and 1 oz. of the grapefruit juice in a blender without ice. Blend well. Pour into a highball glass. Add ice. Add grapefruit juice and stir thoroughly.

Brave Bull

2 oz.   tequila
1 oz.   coffee liqueur

Pour ingredients into an old-fashioned glass almost filled with ice. Stir well.

Rosita

1½ oz. tequila
1 oz.   Campari
½ oz.   dry vermouth
½ oz.   sweet vermouth
        crushed ice

Pour ingredients into an old-fashioned glass nearly filled with crushed ice. Stir well. Serve with a lemon twist.

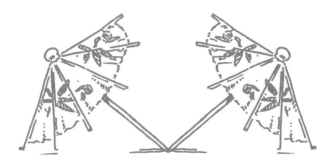

Mexican Madras

1 oz.	gold tequila
1 oz.	orange juice
3 oz.	cranberry juice
splash	lime juice

Combine ingredients in a shaker half filled with ice. Shake well. Strain into an old-fashioned glass over ice.

Mild Madras
(Non-alcoholic)

4 oz.	cranberry juice
4 oz.	orange juice
squeeze	lime

Pour juices into a mixing glass nearly filled with ice. Stir. Strain into a highball glass over ice. Add a squeeze of lime.

Tequila Mockingbird

1½ oz.	tequila
1 oz.	white crème de menthe
1 oz.	lime juice or juice of ½ lime

Combine ingredients in a shaker half filled with ice. Shake well. Strain into a cocktail glass.

Toreador

1½ oz.	tequila
½ oz.	crème de cacao
1 Tbs.	cream

Combine ingredients in a shaker half filled with ice. Shake well. Strain into a cocktail glass.

Tequila Canyon

1½ oz.	tequila
¼ oz.	Triple Sec
3 oz.	cranberry juice
½ oz.	pineapple juice
½ oz.	orange juice

Pour tequila, Triple Sec, and cranberry juice into a collins or highball glass with ice. Add pineapple and orange juices. Serve with a straw.

Tequila Meadow
(Non-alcoholic)

2 oz.	orange juice
2 oz.	pineapple juice
½ oz.	cranberry juice
2 oz.	lemon and lime soda
¼ oz.	grenadine

Combine ingredients except soda in a shaker half filled with ice. Shake well. Strain into a collins glass over ice. Add soda. Stir gently. Garnish with fruit.

Downsider

1½ oz.	tequila
½ oz.	crème de banane
½ oz.	Galliano
1 oz.	cream
1 tsp.	grenadine

Combine ingredients in a shaker half filled with ice. Shake well. Strain into a cocktail glass.

Prairie Fire Shooter

| 1½ oz. | tequila |
| | Tabasco sauce to fill |

Combine ingredients in a mixing glass half filled with ice. Stir. Serve straight up in a shot glass.

C. C. Kazi Shooter

1 oz.	tequila
2 oz.	cranberry juice
1 tsp.	lime juice

Combine ingredients in a shaker half filled with ice. Shake well. Strain into a cordial glass.

MARGARITA ON MY MIND
. . . .

"To salt or not to salt" may be your question, but it's not Margarita's. A classic Margarita (the frozen versions are found in the frozen drink section) is made with the rim of the glass salted: Sprinkle rock salt in a dish. Rub the rim of the glass with a lime wedge. Coat the rim by dipping it into the salt. The zing of the salt and the sweet-tart drink are what make Margaritas memorable.

Margarita

1½ oz.	tequila
1 oz.	lime juice or the juice of ½ lime
½ oz.	Triple Sec
	salt and lime wedge to rim glass

Combine ingredients in a shaker half filled with ice. Shake well. Strain into a salt rimmed cocktail glass. Garnish with a lime wedge. Margaritas can also be served over ice in an old-fashioned glass.

Blue Margarita

1½ oz.	tequila
½ oz.	blue Curaçao
1 tsp.	Triple Sec
1 oz.	lime juice or
	juice of ½ lime
	salt and lime wedge
	to rim glass

Combine ingredients in a shaker half filled with ice. Shake well. Strain into a salt rimmed cocktail glass. Garnish with a lime wedge.

Peach Margarita

1½ oz.	tequila
1 oz.	peach liqueur
1 tsp.	Triple Sec
1 oz.	lime juice or
	juice of ½ lime
	salt and lime wedge
	to rim glass

Combine ingredients in a shaker half filled with ice. Shake well. Strain into a salt rimmed cocktail glass. Garnish with a lime wedge.

WELL-BRED BRANDY

Brandy to the uninitiated can be a bit intimidating. Are a tone of reverence and a crystal snifter required? Definitely not. But a fine brandy is certainly worthy of respect. When the term "brandy" stands alone it refers to a spirit made from grape wine. It's as simple as that.

Almost. The finest brandy comes from the Cognac region of France and bears that name. The length of the aging process of this brandy varies and distillers offer a guide for the buyer. "V.S.," for example, means "very special" according to the following ledger: Very, Special, Old, Pale, Fine, XO(extra old). The initials stand for the number of years the spirit is aged, the longer the better. To further complicate the issue, there are stars to indicate quality, such as a "Five Star" brandy. And the French government has similar designations: Napoleon, Extra, Vieille Reserve, and Vieux. In addition, there is another, more pungent French brandy, Armagnac, named for the region in which it is produced.

Finally, the vintners of California distill brandies from their own grapes, which tend to be lighter and smoother. There is a dry, Italian brandy called Grappa and two Greek varieties, Metaxa, sweet and dark, and Ouzo, with a licorice taste.

There are also fruit brandies such as Apple Brandy or Calvados, as the French version is called; Kirsch or Kirschwasser, made from cherries; Poire William, from pears; Frambois, from raspberries; Frais, from strawberries; and Slivovitz, from plums. These, which are distilled directly from fruit, are true brandies. Other fruit-flavored "brandies" may actually be liqueurs created from a variety of liquors. They are not necessarily inferior, just not made directly from fruit or grape wine. And that's it.

To truly enjoy a fine brandy, it is lovely to drink it from a snifter. Hold the glass in the palm of your hand with the stem between your fingers. That way your body heat will warm the liquor, bringing out its wonderful bouquet and making the most of a rich experience.

B & B

½ oz.	brandy
½ oz.	Benedictine

Pour the Benedictine into a cordial glass. Float the brandy on top.

Metropolitan

1½ oz.	brandy
1 oz.	sweet vermouth
1 tsp.	fine sugar
dash	bitters

Combine in a mixing glass half filled with ice. Stir. Strain into a cocktail glass.

Dream Cocktail

2 oz.	brandy
½ oz.	Triple Sec
1 tsp.	Anisette

Combine ingredients in a shaker nearly filled with ice. Strain into a cocktail glass.

Calvados Cocktail

1½ oz.	Calvados (apple brandy)
2 oz.	orange juice
dash	Triple Sec
	twist of orange peel

Combine ingredients in a shaker nearly filled with ice. Strain into a cocktail glass. Serve with an orange twist.

Brandy Cassis

1½ oz.	brandy
¼ oz.	crème de cassis
1 oz.	lemon juice or juice of ½ lemon

Combine ingredients in a shaker nearly filled with ice. Strain into a cocktail glass. Serve with a lemon twist.

Bombay Cocktail

1 oz.	brandy
½ oz.	dry vermouth
½ oz.	sweet vermouth
½ oz.	Triple Sec

Pour ingredients into a mixing glass nearly filled with ice. Stir. Strain into a cocktail glass. Serve with a lemon twist.

Fancy Brandy

2 oz.	brandy
1/4 oz.	Cointreau
1/4 tsp.	fine sugar
dash	bitters

Pour ingredients into a mixing glass nearly filled with ice. Stir. Strain into a cocktail glass. Serve with a lemon twist.

Brandy Vermouth Classic

2 oz.	brandy
1/2 oz.	sweet vermouth
dash	bitters

Combine ingredients in a mixing glass half filled with ice. Stir. Strain into a cocktail glass.

Brandy Alexander

1 1/2 oz.	brandy
1 oz.	dark crème de cacao
1 oz.	cream
	nutmeg

Combine ingredients in a shaker nearly filled with ice. Strain into a cocktail glass. Garnish with nutmeg.

Creamy Mocha Alexander

1 oz.	coffee liqueur
1 oz.	dark crème de cacao
1 oz.	brandy
2 scoops	ice cream

Put all ingredients in a blender and blend without ice. Pour into a collins or parfait glass. Serve with a straw.

Easy Alexander (Non-alcoholic)

1 tsp.	instant coffee
1 oz.	boiling water
1 tsp.	brown sugar
1 oz.	cream
	nutmeg

Dissolve coffee and sugar in water. Let cool. Combine with cream in a shaker half filled with ice. Shake well. Strain into a cocktail glass. Dust with nutmeg.

Nicky Finn

1 oz.	brandy
1 oz.	Cointreau
1 oz.	lemon juice or juice of 1/2 lemon
dash	Pernod

Combine ingredients in a mixing glass half filled with ice. Stir. Strain into a cocktail glass.

Apple Tart Shooter

| 1 oz. | apple brandy or Calvados |
| 1 oz. | Amaretto |

Pour ingredients into a mixing glass half filled with ice. Stir. Strain into a shot glass.

Scooter Shooter

1 oz.	brandy
1 oz.	Amaretto
1 oz.	light cream

Pour ingredients into a shaker nearly filled with ice. Shake. Strain into a cordial glass.

Angel's Wing Shooter

½ oz.	white crème de cacao
½ oz.	brandy
1 Tbs.	light cream

Pour crème de cacao, brandy, and cream into a cordial glass in that order. Ingredients should be layered.

Jack Rose

1½ oz.	apple brandy
1 oz.	lime juice or juice of ½ lime
½ oz.	grenadine

Combine ingredients in a shaker nearly filled with ice. Strain into a cocktail glass.

Sidecar

1 oz.	brandy
½ oz.	Cointreau
1 oz.	lemon juice or juice of ½ lemon

Combine ingredients in a shaker nearly filled with ice. Strain into a cocktail glass.

. . . .

Brandy: When and Where

. . . .

Of all the spirits, brandy is one that is both versatile and specialized. All brandies, especially the fruited ones, are used in mixed drinks of many kinds. Brandies are also the liquor of choice in the kitchen. Excellent for flaming, they leave a concentration of flavor after the alcohol burns off. Brandies are delightful poured over fresh fruit, cakes, and ice cream. And the cocktail hour would be missing a great deal without brandy.

But the true hour of brandy, on its own, is after dinner. When chatter turns to conversation, when the conviviality of a meal eases into relaxation, brandy is perfect. Some people prefer brandy and soda for a long, refreshing drink. Traditionally, brandy is often served with water, either added to the glass, or served on the side. As the culmination to a meal, brandy is excellent in coffee. Finally, brandy alone, served in a snifter, with its distinctive flavor and remarkable aroma, is the drink of the moment after dinner.

. . . .

RUM: THE COLORFUL ONE

Beginning in the 1600s, members of the British Royal Navy received a half pint of rum a day to ward off scurvy. It didn't work (scurvy is caused by a vitamin C deficiency), but Britannia did rule the oceans for many years. The smooth taste those sailors enjoyed flows from sugar cane, the source of rum. Rum varies from light to dark in color. The clear and pale gold versions are characteristically lighter in taste. The darker, which range from amber to chestnut, are heavier and richer in flavor. Puerto Rico is often the source for the lighter liquor; Jamaica, Haiti, and Martinique for the darker. Both are about 80 proof. There are 151 proof rums, fine for flaming and a few specialty drinks, but twice as potent and inappropriate when lifting a glass to enjoy the fine, mellow taste of rum.

Cuba Libre or Rum and Coke

| 2 oz. | light rum |
| 6 oz. | cola |

Pour rum and cola into a highball glass over ice. Garnish with a lime wedge.

Lime Cola (Non-alcoholic)

| 1 oz. | lime juice or juice of ½ lime |
| | cola to fill |

Pour over ice in a highball glass. Garnish with a lime wedge.

Cherry Coke (Non-alcoholic)

2 oz.	grenadine
	cola to fill
	maraschino cherry

Pour over ice in a highball glass. Garnish with a cherry.

Blue Marlin Shooter

1 oz.	light rum
½ oz.	blue Curaçao
1 oz.	lime juice

Pour ingredients into a mixing glass half filled with ice. Stir. Strain into a shot glass.

Boston Sidecar

1 oz.	light rum
½ oz.	brandy
¾ oz.	Triple Sec
1 oz.	lime juice or juice of ½ lime

Combine ingredients in a shaker nearly filled with ice. Strain into a cocktail glass.

Continental

1½ oz.	light rum
½ oz.	green crème de menthe
½ tsp.	fine sugar
1 Tbs.	lime juice
1 tsp.	lemon juice

Combine ingredients in a shaker nearly filled with ice. Strain into a cocktail glass. Serve with a lemon twist.

Corkscrew

1½ oz.	light rum
½ oz.	peach-flavored brandy
½ oz.	dry vermouth

Combine ingredients in a shaker nearly filled with ice. Strain into a cocktail glass. Serve with a lemon twist.

Pineapple Mist

| 2 oz. | light rum |
| 3 oz. | pineapple juice |

Combine rum and juice in a blender with ice and blend thoroughly. Pour into a cocktail glass and serve with a cherry.

Pineapple Twist (Non-alcoholic)

4 oz.	pineapple juice
1 oz.	lemon juice or juice of ½ lemon
2 oz.	orange juice or juice of ½ orange

Combine juices in a blender with ice and blend thoroughly. Pour into a cocktail glass and serve with a cherry.

Bacardi Cocktail

1½ oz.	Bacardi rum
1 oz.	lime juice or juice of ½ lime
½ tsp.	grenadine

Combine all ingredients in a shaker half filled with ice. Shake well. Strain into a cocktail glass.

El Chico

1½ oz.	light rum
½ oz.	sweet vermouth
¼ tsp.	grenadine
¼ tsp.	Curaçao

Combine ingredients in a shaker nearly filled with ice. Strain into a cocktail glass. Serve with a cherry and lemon twist.

Bolo

2 oz.	light rum
1 oz.	lime juice or juice of ½ lime
1 oz.	orange juice
1 tsp.	fine sugar

Combine ingredients in a shaker nearly filled with ice. Strain into a cocktail glass.

Bolero

1½ oz.	light rum
¾ oz.	Calvados or apple brandy
1 tsp.	sweet vermouth

Combine ingredients in a mixing glass half filled with ice. Stir well. Pour into an old-fashioned glass with ice.

El Presidenté

1½ oz	light rum
1 oz.	lime juice or juice of ½ lime
½ oz.	pineapple juice
1 tsp.	grenadine

Combine ingredients in a shaker nearly filled with ice. Strain into a cocktail glass.

Vice Presidenté (Non-alcoholic)

2 oz.	pineapple juice
1 oz.	lime juice or juice of ½ lime
½ oz.	grenadine
1 tsp.	fine sugar

Combine ingredients in a shaker nearly filled with ice. Strain into a cocktail glass.

Reno Cocktail (Non-alcoholic)

2 oz.	grapefruit juice
1 oz.	lime juice or juice of ½ lime
½ oz.	grenadine
1 tsp.	fine sugar

Combine ingredients in a shaker nearly filled with ice. Strain into a cocktail glass.

Golden Friendship

1 oz.	light rum
1 oz.	sweet vermouth
1 oz.	Amaretto
4 oz.	ginger ale

Pour rum, vermouth, and Amaretto into a collins glass with ice. Add ginger ale. Garnish with a cherry.

Apple Pie

1 oz.	rum
½ oz.	sweet vermouth
1 tsp.	apple brandy
1 oz.	lemon juice or juice of ½ lemon
½ tsp.	grenadine

Combine all ingredients in a shaker half filled with ice. Shake well. Strain into a cocktail glass.

Black Maria

2 oz.	light rum
1 oz.	coffee-flavored brandy
3 oz.	strong black coffee
2 tsp.	fine sugar

Pour all ingredients into a brandy snifter and stir. Add ice.

PART III
MIXED DRINKS— CLASSIC AND CURRENT

Sours, Collins, Gimlets, Rickeys, Fizzes, Old-Fashioneds, Fixes, Coolers, Cobblers, Screwdrivers, Smashes, Swizzles, Slings, Juleps, Stingers, Martinis, Manhattans, Bloody Marys, Daisys

THE SOUR

The sweetness of sugar and the tartness of
lemon are the lure of the Sour. The alchemy of
the combination is its secret. For convenience,
you can choose a sour mix. But for a superior
cocktail, try mixing your own with fresh lemon
juice and powdered sugar. This drink is a basic
shaken cocktail, so get out your shaker and
strainer, and experience the true tanginess of a
Sour.

The Whiskey Sour is the mother of all
sours, but substitutes for whiskey can be
bourbon, rum, tequila, vodka, or
brandy.

Serve in a
stemmed sour
glass. A Sour on the
rocks is poured over ice
into an old-fashioned glass.

Whiskey Sour

2 oz.	blended whiskey
1 oz.	lemon juice or juice of ½ lemon
1 tsp.	fine sugar (or 1½ oz. sour mix instead of lemon and sugar)

Fill shaker glass two-thirds with ice. Add ingredients. Shake. Strain into sour glass. Garnish with lemon and a cherry.

Scotch Sour

2 oz.	scotch
1 oz.	lime juice or juice of ½ lime
1 tsp.	fine sugar

Shake ingredients. Strain into a sour glass. Garnish with an orange slice and cherry. Note that lime juice instead of lemon juice means sour mix is nixed.

Egg Sour

2 oz.	brandy
1 tsp.	Cointreau
½ oz.	lemon juice
1	egg

Fill shaker glass two-thirds with ice. Add ingredients. Shake. Strain into a sour glass.

Fireman's Sour

2 oz.	light rum
2 oz.	lime juice or juice of one lime
1 Tbs.	grenadine
1 tsp.	fine sugar
	club soda

Pour all ingredients except the club soda into a shaker with ice. Shake well. Strain into a sour glass and fill with club soda. Garnish with a lemon slice and cherry.

Brandy Sour

2 oz.	brandy
1 oz.	lemon juice or juice of ½ lemon
1 tsp.	fine sugar (or 1½ oz. sour mix instead of lemon and sugar)

Fill shaker glass two-thirds with ice. Add ingredients. Shake. Strain into a sour glass. Garnish with lemon and a cherry.

Double Standard Sour

1 oz.	blended whiskey
1 oz.	gin
	juice of $1/2$ lemon
	or lime
1 tsp.	fine sugar
$1/2$ tsp.	grenadine

Fill shaker glass two-thirds with ice. Add ingredients. Shake. Strain into a sour glass. Garnish with lemon and a cherry.

Frisco Sour

2 oz.	blended whiskey
$1/2$ oz.	Benedictine
$1/2$ oz.	lemon juice
$1/2$ oz.	lime juice
$1/2$ tsp.	fine sugar

Fill shaker glass two-thirds with ice. Add ingredients. Shake. Strain into a sour glass. Garnish with lemon and a cherry.

Gin Sour

2 oz.	gin
1 oz.	lemon juice or
	juice of $1/2$ lemon
1 tsp.	fine sugar
	(or $1 1/2$ oz. sour mix
	instead of lemon
	and sugar)

Fill shaker glass two-thirds with ice. Add ingredients. Shake. Strain into a sour glass. Garnish with lemon and a cherry.

Rum Sour

2 oz.	rum
1 oz.	lemon juice or
	juice of $1/2$ lemon
1 tsp.	fine sugar
	(or $1 1/2$ oz. sour mix
	instead of lemon
	and sugar)

Fill shaker glass two-thirds with ice. Add ingredients. Shake. Strain into a sour glass. Garnish with lemon and a cherry.

Tequila Sour

2 oz.	tequila
1 oz.	lemon juice or juice of ½ lemon
1 tsp.	fine sugar (or 1½ oz. sour mix instead of lemon and sugar)

Fill shaker glass two-thirds with ice. Add ingredients. Shake. Strain into a sour glass. Garnish with lemon and a cherry.

Vodka Sour

2 oz.	vodka
1 oz.	lemon juice or juice of ½ lemon
1 tsp.	fine sugar (or 1½ oz. sour mix instead of lemon and sugar)

Fill shaker glass two-thirds with ice. Add ingredients. Shake. Strain into a sour glass. Garnish with lemon and a cherry.

Amaretto Sour

| 1½ oz. | Amaretto |
| 1 oz. | Rose's lime juice |

Fill shaker glass two-thirds with ice. Add ingredients. Shake. Strain into a sour glass. Garnish with lemon and a cherry.

Applejack Sour

2 oz.	apple brandy
½ oz.	lemon juice
1 tsp.	fine sugar

Combine with ice in a shaker. Shake well. Pour into a sour glass.

Sweet and Sour Apple (Non-alcoholic)

2 oz.	apple juice
½ oz.	lemon juice
1 tsp.	fine sugar
1	egg white

Fill shaker glass two-thirds with ice. Add ingredients. Shake well. Strain and pour into a sour glass. Garnish with an orange slice and a cherry.

THE COLLINS FAMILY

Think of a Collins as a sour with a touch of the bubbly—club soda—over ice. A Tom Collins, made with gin, is a classic. John Collins, created with whiskey, follows the pattern, along with Vodka Collins, Rum Collins, and Tequila Collins. This elegant family is served in its namesake glass, the collins, a frosted highball glass.

Tom Cat Collins (Non-alcoholic)

2 oz.	lemon juice or juice of 1 lemon
1 Tbs.	fine sugar or to taste
5	mint leaves club soda or sparkling water

Combine mint leaves with lemon and sugar in a collins glass. Crush with a spoon. Add soda. Garnish with a lemon slice.

Tom Collins

2 oz.	gin
1 oz.	lemon juice or juice of $\frac{1}{2}$ lemon
1 tsp.	fine sugar
3 oz.	club soda

. . . .

John Collins

2 oz.	blended whiskey
1 oz.	lemon juice or juice of $\frac{1}{2}$ lemon
1 tsp.	fine sugar
3 oz.	club soda

. . . .

Jock Collins

2 oz.	scotch
1 oz.	lemon juice or juice of $\frac{1}{2}$ lemon
1 tsp.	fine sugar
3 oz.	club soda

. . . .

Vodka Collins

2 oz.	vodka
1 oz.	lemon juice or juice of $\frac{1}{2}$ lemon
1 tsp.	fine sugar
3 oz.	club soda

Rum Collins

2 oz.	rum
1 oz.	lemon juice or juice of $\frac{1}{2}$ lemon
1 tsp.	fine sugar
3 oz.	club soda

. . . .

Tequila Collins

2 oz.	tequila
1 oz.	lemon juice or juice of $\frac{1}{2}$ lemon
1 tsp.	fine sugar
3 oz.	club soda

. . . .

Whiskey Collins

2 oz.	whiskey
1 oz.	lemon juice or juice of $\frac{1}{2}$ lemon
1 tsp.	fine sugar
3 oz.	club soda

. . . .

For all of these individual recipes, combine the liquor, lemon juice, and sugar in a shaker half filled with ice. Shake well. Strain into a collins glass nearly filled with ice. Add club soda. Stir. Garnish with a cherry and orange slice. Can be served with a straw.

THE GIMLET: A BOUQUET OF ROSE'S

Rose's lime juice, which is concentrated and sweetened, was first introduced to the world as a remedy for scurvy. But how much more delightful it is combined with gin to create a Gimlet. Rose's is imported from England and makes the quintessential Gimlet. *Very* British. Rum, vodka, and tequila also make delicious, but decidedly *un*-British Gimlets.

Gimlet

2 oz.   gin
1/2 oz. Rose's lime juice (or
         1 oz. lime juice and
         1 tsp. fine sugar)

The gimlet is a stirred cocktail made in a shaker (or mixing glass) half filled with ice. Pour the lime juice and gin into the mixing glass. Stir well. Strain into a cocktail glass. Garnish with a lime wedge.

Vodka Gimlet

2 oz.   vodka
1/2 oz. Rose's lime juice (or
         1 oz. lime juice and
         1 tsp. fine sugar)

Add all ingredients to a mixing glass half filled with ice. Stir. Strain into a cocktail glass. Garnish with a lime wedge.

Rum Gimlet

2 oz.   rum
1/2 oz. Rose's lime juice (or
         1 oz. lime juice and
         1 tsp. fine sugar)

Add all ingredients to a mixing glass half filled with ice. Stir. Strain into a cocktail glass. Garnish with a lime wedge.

Tequila Gimlet

2 oz.   tequila
1/2 oz. Rose's lime juice (or
         1 oz. lime juice and
         1 tsp. fine sugar)

Add all ingredients to a mixing glass half filled with ice. Stir. Strain into a cocktail glass. Garnish with a lime wedge.

Goody-Goody Gimlet (Non-alcoholic)

3 oz.   lime juice or
         juice of 1 1/2 limes
2 tsp.   fine sugar
5 oz.   ice water

In a highball glass, dissolve sugar in lime juice. Add ice. Fill with water. Stir. Garnish with a slice of lime.

RICKEY, MEET GIMLET

A Rickey is made with any liquor combined with club soda and the tantalizing snap of lime. The "Lime Rickey" or "Rickey Gimlet" is actually a fizzy Gimlet courtesy of the club soda. It is built on the classic taste of the Gimlet which already contains the tang of Rose's lime juice.

Righteous Rickey (Non-alcoholic)

1 Tbs.   Rose's lime juice
5 oz.   club soda

Pour lime juice into a highball glass over ice. Fill with club soda. Stir. Garnish with a slice of lime.

Apricot Brandy Rickey

2 oz.   apricot brandy
1 oz.   lime juice or
         juice of ½ lime
4 oz.   club soda

Pour brandy and lime juice into a highball glass nearly filled with ice. Add club soda. Stir. Serve with a twist of lime.

Lime Rickey

1½ oz.   gin
1½ oz.   Rose's lime juice
4 oz.   club soda

Pour the gin and lime juice into a highball glass nearly filled with ice. Stir gently. Add club soda. Garnish with a twist of lime.

Apple Brandy Rickey

1½ oz.   apple brandy
1 oz.   lime juice or
             juice of ½ lime
             club soda

Pour the apple brandy and lime juice into a highball glass nearly filled with ice. Stir gently. Add club soda. Garnish with a twist of lime.

Rum Rickey

1½ oz.   rum
1 oz.   lime juice or
             juice of ½ lime
             club soda

Pour the rum and lime juice into a highball glass nearly filled with ice. Stir gently. Add club soda. Garnish with a twist of lime.

Scotch Rickey

1½ oz.   scotch
1 oz.   lime juice or
             juice of ½ lime
             club soda

Pour the scotch and lime juice into a highball glass nearly filled with ice. Stir. Add club soda. Garnish with a twist of lime.

Irish Rickey

1½ oz.   blended whiskey
1 oz.   lime juice or
             juice of ½ lime
             club soda

Pour the whiskey and lime juice into a highball glass nearly filled with ice. Stir. Add club soda. Garnish with a twist of lime.

Kirsch Rickey

2 oz.   kirschwasser
1 Tbs.   lime juice
             club soda

Pour kirschwasser and lime juice into a highball glass nearly filled with ice. Add club soda. Stir gently. Garnish with a cherry.

THE FIZZ : BEYOND SLOE GIN

The Fizz gets its fizziness from club soda and its romance from the famous Sloe Gin Fizz, a creation that conjures up visions of languid ladies and side-long glances. Brandy, apricot brandy, and gin make splendid Fizzes. For a personal Fizz, try adding any liquor of choice.

Sloe Gin Fizz

2 oz.	sloe gin
1 oz.	lemon juice or juice of ½ lemon
1 tsp.	fine sugar
4 oz.	club soda

Combine the lemon juice, sugar, and liquor in a shaker half filled with ice. Shake well. Pour into a highball glass partly filled with ice and add club soda. Stir and garnish with lemon.

Imperial Fizz

1 oz.	light rum
1 oz.	blended whiskey
1 oz.	lemon juice or juice of ½ lemon
1 tsp.	fine sugar
4 oz.	club soda

Combine the lemon juice, sugar, and liquor in a shaker half filled with ice. Shake well. Pour into a highball glass partly filled with ice and add club soda. Stir and garnish with lemon.

Apricot Fizz

2 oz.	apricot-flavored brandy
1 oz.	lemon juice or juice of ½ lemon
1 oz.	lime juice or juice of ½ lime
1 tsp.	fine sugar
4 oz.	club soda

Combine the juices, sugar, and liquor in a shaker half filled with ice. Shake well. Pour into a highball glass partly filled with ice and add club soda. Stir and garnish with lemon.

Pineapple Fizz

2 oz.	light rum
1 oz.	pineapple juice
1 tsp.	fine sugar
	club soda

Combine the juice, sugar, and liquor in a shaker half filled with ice. Shake well. Pour into a highball glass partly filled with ice and add club soda. Stir and garnish with lemon.

Gin or
Alabama Fizz

2 oz.	gin
1 oz.	lemon juice or juice of $^1/_2$ lemon
1 tsp.	fine sugar
4 oz.	club soda

Combine the lemon juice, sugar, and liquor in a shaker half filled with ice. Shake well. Pour into a highball glass partly filled with ice and add club soda. Stir and garnish with lemon.

Brandy Fizz

2 oz.	brandy
1 oz.	lemon juice or juice of $^1/_2$ lemon
1 tsp.	fine sugar
4 oz.	club soda

Combine the lemon juice, sugar, and liquor in a shaker half filled with ice. Shake well. Pour into a highball glass partly filled with ice and add club soda. Stir and garnish with lemon.

Cherry Fizz

2 oz.	cherry brandy
1 oz.	lemon juice or juice of $^1/_2$ lemon
4 oz.	club soda

Combine the lemon juice, liquor, and sugar in a shaker half filled with ice. Shake well. Pour into a highball glass partly filled with ice. Stir and garnish with a cherry.

Jubilee Fizz

2 oz.	gin
1 oz.	lemon juice or juice of $^1/_2$ lemon
$^1/_2$ tsp.	fine sugar
4 oz.	chilled champagne

Combine the lemon juice, liquor, and sugar in a shaker half filled with ice. Shake well. Pour into a highball glass partly filled with ice. Stir.

Royal Fizz

2 oz.	gin
1 oz.	orange juice or juice of ½ orange
1 oz.	lemon juice or juice of ½ lemon
1 tsp.	fine sugar
1 tsp.	Cointreau
2 tsp.	light cream

Combine all ingredients in a shaker half filled with ice. Shake well. Pour into a highball glass partly filled with ice and add club soda. Stir and garnish with fruit.

Vineyard Fizz
(Non-alcoholic)

2 oz.	grape juice
1 oz.	lemon juice or juice of ½ lemon
½ tsp.	fine sugar
	cream soda

Combine the grape juice, lemon juice, and sugar in a shaker half filled with ice. Shake well. Pour into a highball glass partly filled with ice. Add soda. Stir gently.

It's Called Old-Fashioned for a Reason

Legend has it that the Old-Fashioned was invented for a civil war general.

Alas, the soldier was on the losing side, but the drink remains a winner. For new-fangled versions, try tequila or rum.

Old-Fashioned

2 oz.	blended whiskey
1 cube or	
½ tsp.	sugar
1 tsp.	water
dash or 2	bitters
	lemon twist

Combine the sugar, bitters, and water in an old-fashioned glass and muddle with a spoon. Pour whiskey and stir. Add ice cubes and a lemon twist. Garnish with a slice of orange or lemon and a cherry.

Bourbon Old-Fashioned

2 oz.	bourbon
1 cube or	
½ tsp.	sugar
1 tsp.	water
dash or 2	bitters
	lemon twist

Combine the sugar, bitters, and water in an old-fashioned glass and muddle with a spoon. Pour bourbon and stir. Add ice cubes and a lemon twist. Garnish with a slice of orange or lemon and a cherry.

Tequila Old-Fashioned

2 oz.	tequila
1 tsp.	water
1 cube or	
½ tsp.	sugar
dash or 2	bitters
	lemon twist

Combine the sugar, bitters, and water in an old-fashioned glass and muddle with a spoon. Pour tequila and stir. Add ice cubes and a lemon twist. Garnish with a slice of orange or lemon and a cherry.

Scotch Old-Fashioned

2 oz.	scotch
1 tsp.	water
1 cube or	
½ tsp.	sugar
dash or 2	bitters
	lemon twist

Combine the sugar, bitters, and water in an old-fashioned glass and muddle with a spoon. Pour scotch and stir. Add ice cubes and a lemon twist. Garnish with a slice of orange or lemon and a cherry.

A Good Fix

A Fix is a cocktail with a lemon tang and the frosty touch of crushed ice. Fix up a Fix for your taste craving of the moment—with bourbon, brandy, gin, rum, scotch, or whiskey. Just fix it.

Rum Fix

2 oz.	light rum
1 oz.	lemon juice or juice of $1/2$ lemon
1 tsp.	fine sugar
2 tsp.	water
	crushed ice

Add sugar, lemon juice, and water to a shaker half filled with ice cubes. Shake. Strain into a highball glass filled with crushed ice. Add liquor. Stir. Garnish with lemon. Serve with a straw.

Gin Fix

2 oz.	gin
1 oz.	lemon juice or juice of $1/2$ lemon
1 tsp.	fine sugar
2 tsp.	water
	crushed ice

Add sugar, lemon juice, and water to a shaker half filled with ice cubes. Shake. Strain into a highball glass filled with crushed ice. Add liquor. Stir. Garnish with lemon. Serve with a straw.

Brandy Fix

2 oz.	brandy
1 oz.	lemon juice or juice of $1/2$ lemon
1 tsp.	fine sugar
2 tsp.	water
	crushed ice

Add sugar, lemon juice, and water to a shaker half filled with ice cubes. Shake. Strain into a highball glass filled with crushed ice. Add liquor. Stir. Garnish with lemon. Serve with a straw.

Whiskey Fix

2 oz.	blended whiskey
1 oz.	lemon juice or juice of $1/2$ lemon
1 tsp.	fine sugar

Add lemon juice and sugar to a shaker half filled with ice. Shake. Strain into a highball glass. Add ice and liquor. Stir. Serve with a straw.

BE COOLER

Coolers are made with a twist of citrus and lots of fizz. An absolute bare-bones cooler can be assembled with 2 oz. of liquor (scotch, gin, rum, bourbon, vodka, tequila, or whiskey) and 4 oz. of club soda or ginger ale poured into a highball glass almost filled with ice. But to be cool, here are a few more cultivated coolers.

Pineapple Cooler
(Non-alcoholic)

4 oz.   pineapple juice
1 tsp.   fine sugar
           club soda

Dissolve sugar in pineapple juice in a highball glass. Add ice. Pour club soda to fill. Stir gently.

Rousing Cooler
(Non-alcoholic)

1 oz.   lime juice or
           juice of ½ lime
           ginger beer

Pour lime juice into a highball or collins glass over ice. Add ginger beer. Stir gently. Garnish with a lime wedge.

Gin Cooler

2 oz.	gin
2 oz.	club soda
1 tsp.	fine sugar
	ginger ale

Dissolve sugar in club soda in a collins glass. Nearly fill the glass with ice. Add gin. Fill with ginger ale. Serve with a fruit slice.

Vodka Cooler

2 oz.	vodka
2 oz.	club soda
1 tsp.	fine sugar
	ginger ale

Dissolve sugar in club soda in a collins glass. Nearly fill the glass with ice. Add vodka. Fill with ginger ale. Serve with a fruit slice.

Rum Cooler

2 oz.	rum
2 oz.	club soda
1 tsp.	fine sugar
	ginger ale

Dissolve sugar in club soda in a collins glass. Nearly fill the glass with ice. Add rum. Fill with ginger ale. Serve with a fruit slice.

Boston Cooler

2 oz.	rum
1 oz.	lemon juice or juice of 1/2 lemon
1 tsp.	fine sugar
3 oz.	club soda or ginger ale
	twist of lemon

Into a highball glass, pour lemon juice, sugar, and a bit of soda. Stir. Nearly fill the glass with ice. Add rum and soda. Stir and complete with a twist of lemon.

Apricot Cooler

2 oz.	apricot brandy
1/2 oz.	grenadine
4 oz.	lemon and lime soda

Fill a highball glass with ice. Pour brandy and grenadine. Stir. Fill with soda.

Scotch Cooler

2 oz.	scotch
Splash	white crème de menthe
3 oz.	club soda
	mint sprigs

Fill a highball glass with ice. Pour scotch and crème de menthe. Fill with soda. Stir. Garnish with mint.

THE COBBLER: A CRUSHED ICE CLASSIC

The Cobbler's lasting appeal is the singular sensation of crushed ice. Strip the Cobbler of its frosty pulverization and it's a Cooler, but the difference is *not* subtle. Crushed ice, crunchy and melting, alters the texture of a drink: its feel, its texture, its moment in the mouth when a drink defines itself and imparts its own very particular pleasure.

Rum Cobbler

2 oz.	dark rum
2 oz.	club soda
1 tsp.	fine sugar
	crushed ice

Pour club soda into a goblet. Add sugar and dissolve. Fill with crushed ice. Add rum and stir. Garnish with fruit and serve with a straw.

Brandy Cobbler

2 oz.	brandy
2 oz.	club soda
1 tsp.	fine sugar
	crushed ice

Pour club soda into a goblet. Add sugar and dissolve. Fill with crushed ice. Add brandy and stir. Garnish with fruit and serve with a straw.

Bourbon Cobbler

2 oz.	bourbon
1 Tbs.	grapefruit juice
1 tsp.	lemon juice
1 tsp.	almond extract
	crushed ice

Combine ingredients in a shaker half filled with ice. Shake well. Strain into an old-fashioned glass filled with crushed ice. Garnish with fruit and serve with a straw.

Gin Cobbler

2 oz.	gin
2 oz.	club soda
1 tsp.	fine sugar
	crushed ice

Pour club soda into a goblet. Add sugar and dissolve. Fill with crushed ice. Add gin and stir. Garnish with fruit and serve with a straw.

Whiskey Cobbler

2 oz.	blended whiskey
2 oz.	club soda
1 tsp.	fine sugar
	crushed ice

Pour club soda into a goblet. Add sugar and dissolve. Fill with crushed ice. Add whiskey and stir. Garnish with fruit and serve with a straw.

Scotch Cobbler

2 oz.	scotch
2 oz.	club soda
1 tsp.	fine sugar
	crushed ice

Pour club soda into a goblet. Add sugar and dissolve. Fill with crushed ice. Add scotch and stir. Garnish with fruit and serve with a straw.

THE SCREWDRIVER: NOT JUST FOR HOME REPAIR

Orange juice graduated from the breakfast table to the bar when it met vodka and became the Screwdriver. The juice also mixes it up with other liquors to make the Rum Screwdriver, the Scotch Screwdriver, and a couple of even screwier drivers.

Italian Screwdriver

1½ oz.	citrus vodka
3 oz.	orange juice
2 oz.	grapefruit juice
splash	ginger ale

Combine all ingredients in a mixing glass. Stir well. Pour into a highball glass and garnish with a slice of fruit.

Slow Comfortable Screw

1½ oz.	vodka
½ oz.	sloe gin
½ oz.	Southern Comfort
4 oz.	orange juice

Pour all ingredients into a highball glass nearly filled with ice. Stir well.

Slow Comfortable Screw Up Against the Wall

1½ oz.	vodka
1 oz.	sloe gin
1 oz.	Southern Comfort
4 oz.	orange juice
1 oz.	Galliano

Pour all ingredients except Galliano into a highball glass nearly filled with ice. Stir well. Float Galliano on top.

Screwdriver

1½ oz.	vodka
5 oz.	orange juice

Pour orange juice and vodka into a highball glass nearly filled with ice. Stir well.

Very Screwy Driver

1 oz.	vodka
½ oz.	gin
½ oz.	tequila
4 oz.	orange juice

Pour all ingredients into a highball glass nearly filled with ice. Stir well.

Creamy Screwdriver

2 oz.	vodka
½ tsp.	fine sugar
1	egg yolk
4 oz.	orange juice

Combine all ingredients in a blender with ice. Blend. Pour into a highball glass with ice.

Screwless Driver (Non-alcoholic)

1½ oz.	tonic water
5 oz.	orange juice

Pour orange juice and tonic into a highball glass nearly filled with ice. Stir well.

BUBBLE UP WITH MINT FOR A SMASH

The refreshing zip of mint and club soda make the Smash a classic. Brandy, whiskey, and gin are the basic liquors. But don't forget to enjoy the smell of mint and the little quiver of bubbles, because that's what makes the Smash a bash.

Brandy Smash

2 oz.	brandy
1 tsp.	fine sugar
4 sprigs	mint
1 oz.	club soda
	lemon twist

Muddle the sugar with mint and club soda in an old-fashioned glass. Fill the glass with ice cubes. Pour brandy. Stir well. Add a twist of lemon.

Gin Smash

2 oz.	gin
1 tsp.	fine sugar
4 sprigs	mint
1 oz.	club soda
	lemon twist

Muddle the sugar with mint and club soda in an old-fashioned glass. Fill the glass with ice cubes. Pour gin. Stir well. Add a twist of lemon.

Whiskey Smash

2 oz.	blended whiskey
1 tsp.	fine sugar
4 sprigs	mint
1 oz.	club soda
	lemon twist

Muddle the sugar with mint and club soda in an old-fashioned glass. Fill the glass with ice cubes. Pour whiskey. Stir well. Add a twist of lemon.

Sprightly Smash (Non-alcoholic)

3 oz.	grapefruit juice
1 tsp.	Rose's lime juice
1 Tbs.	fine sugar
4 sprigs	mint, chopped
	club soda

Combine juices and sugar in a saucepan and bring to a boil. Add mint leaves and cool. Strain into a highball or collins glass over ice. Add soda to fill. Garnish with mint.

A SWIZZLE IS NOT JUST A STICK

A Swizzle is a cocktail that combines the benefits of a good shake,

the pucker of bitters,

and the tingle of club soda. Bourbon, brandy, gin, rum, scotch, and whiskey can all be swizzled.

Gringo Swizzle

2 oz.	tequila
1/2 oz.	crème de cassis
1 oz.	lime juice or juice of 1/2 lime
1 oz.	orange juice
1 oz.	pineapple juice
1 tsp.	fine sugar ginger ale, chilled

Combine all ingredients except ginger ale in a shaker half filled with ice. Shake well. Strain into a collins or highball glass. Fill with ginger ale.

Whiskey Swizzle

2 oz.	whiskey
1½ oz.	lime juice or juice of 1 lime
1 tsp.	fine sugar
2 dashes	bitters
3 oz.	club soda
	crushed ice

Combine the lime juice, sugar, liquor, and bitters in a shaker half filled with ice. Shake well. Strain into a collins glass almost filled with crushed ice. Stir. Fill with soda. Serve with a swizzle stick.

Gin Swizzle

2 oz.	gin
1½ oz.	lime juice or juice of 1 lime
1 tsp.	fine sugar
2 dashes	bitters
3 oz.	club soda
	crushed ice

Combine the lime juice, sugar, liquor, and bitters in a shaker half filled with ice. Shake well. Strain into a collins glass almost filled with crushed ice. Stir. Fill with soda. Serve with a swizzle stick.

Sunny Swizzle
(Non-alcoholic)

3 oz.	mixed juice like banana-strawberry
1½ oz.	lime juice or juice of 1 lime
1 tsp.	fine sugar
1 dash	orange bitters
3 oz.	club soda
	crushed ice

Combine the juices, sugar, and bitters in a shaker half filled with ice. Shake well. Strain into a collins glass almost filled with crushed ice. Stir. Fill with soda. Serve with a swizzle stick.

Brandy Swizzle

2 oz.	brandy
1½ oz.	lime juice or juice of 1 lime
1 tsp.	fine sugar
2 dashes	bitters
3 oz.	club soda
	crushed ice

Combine the lime juice, sugar, liquor, and bitters in a shaker half filled with ice. Shake well. Strain into a collins glass almost filled with crushed ice. Stir. Fill with soda. Serve with a swizzle stick.

THE SLING: SINGAPORE AND BEYOND

The Sling is a basic drink made famous by its exotic Singaporean cousin, said to have been invented at the famous Raffles Hotel in Singapore. Cherry brandy is its intriguing ingredient. However, ordinary brandy, whiskey, scotch, and vodka create tasty alternatives.

Singapore Sling

1 oz.	gin
1/2 oz.	cherry brandy
1 tsp.	fine sugar
4 oz.	club soda
	fruit slices

Combine the liquor, lemon juice, sugar, and gin in a shaker half filled with ice. Shake well. Strain into a collins glass nearly filled with ice cubes. Fill with club soda. Float cherry brandy on top. Garnish with an orange or lemon slice. Serve with a straw.

Celibate Sling
(Non-alcoholic)

4 oz.	cherry soda
2 oz.	ginger ale
splash	lemon juice
1 tsp.	grenadine

Pour cherry soda, ginger ale, and lemon juice into a collins glass. Stir. Float grenadine on top. Garnish with fruit. Serve with a straw.

Whiskey Sling

2 oz.	blended whiskey
1 oz.	lemon juice or juice of ½ lemon
1 tsp.	water
1 tsp.	fine sugar
	lemon twist

. . . .

Vodka Sling

2 oz.	vodka
1 oz.	lemon juice or juice of ½ lemon
1 tsp.	water
1 tsp.	fine sugar
	lemon twist

. . . .

Gin Sling

2 oz.	gin
1 oz.	lemon juice or juice of ½ lemon
1 tsp.	water
1 tsp.	fine sugar
	lemon twist.

Brandy Sling

2 oz.	brandy
1 oz.	lemon juice or juice of ½ lemon
1 tsp.	water
1 tsp.	fine sugar
	lemon twist

. . . .

Highland Sling

2 oz.	scotch
1 oz.	lemon juice or juice of ½ lemon
1 tsp.	water
1 tsp.	fine sugar
	lemon twist.

. . . .

For all of these individual recipes, combine the liquor, lemon juice, sugar, and water in a shaker half filled with ice. Shake well. Strain into an old-fashioned glass over ice. Stir. Add the twist of lemon.

MORE THAN A MINT JULEP

The first Saturday in May is the Kentucky Derby and always the day to toast your sweetheart with a Mint Julep. This drink even has its own silver "julep cup," but a highball or collins glass will do. Bourbon is the classic choice, but there are a few variations for those willing to subvert such an august tradition. There is some controversy about whether to muddle the mint leaves, but mint is essential. Muddled or garnishing the glass, mint is the southern soul of the Julep. So pick a horse and toast the winner, but always with a Mint Julep.

Mint Julep

2½ oz.	bourbon
1 tsp.	fine sugar
1 tsp.	water
4 sprigs	mint
	crushed ice

In a collins glass, muddle the mint leaves, sugar, and water. Fill the glass with crushed ice and add the bourbon. Garnish with mint and serve with straws.

Georgia Mint Julep

1 oz.	brandy
1 oz.	peach-flavored brandy
1 tsp.	fine sugar
2 sprigs	mint
splash	water

Muddle the mint, sugar, and water in an old-fashioned glass. Add ice. Pour brandy and liqueur into the glass. Stir.

Champagne Julep

2 oz.	bourbon
4 oz.	champagne
1 tsp.	fine sugar
1 tsp.	water
4 sprigs	mint

In a mixing glass, muddle the mint, water, and sugar. Add bourbon. Strain into a collins glass. Add ice cubes. Pour in champagne. Garnish with mint.

Juicy Julep
(Non-alcoholic)

1 oz.	lime juice or juice of ½ lime
1 oz.	orange juice
1 oz.	pineapple juice
½ oz.	raspberry syrup
	club soda to fill the glass
4	crushed mint leaves.

Combine all ingredients except club soda in a shaker half filled with ice. Shake well. Strain into a collins glass. Add club soda and stir gently. Garnish with a sprig of mint.

STINGERS, GRASSHOPPERS, AND OTHER BUGS

Open a bottle of white crème de menthe.

See any bugs?

Well, they're in
there. Grasshoppers
and Stingers and Spiders
are all made with crème de menthe. The
proportions of liquor to crème de menthe in the
drinks that follow is generally one to one. But
taste should prevail. For a sweeter drink,
decrease the amount of liquor and increase the
amount of crème de menthe. And don't let the
bugs bite.

Stinger

| 2 oz. | B & B or five star brandy |
| 2 oz. | white crème de menthe |

Pour ingredients into a mixing glass nearly filled with ice. Stir. Strain into a cocktail glass. A stinger on the rocks is served in an old-fashioned glass with ice.

Vodka Stinger

| 2 oz. | vodka |
| 2 oz. | white crème de menthe |

Pour ingredients into a mixing glass nearly filled with ice. Stir. Strain into a cocktail glass.

Galliano Stinger

| 2 oz. | Galliano |
| 2 oz. | white crème de menthe |

Pour ingredients into a mixing glass nearly filled with ice. Stir. Strain into a cocktail glass.

Scotch Stinger

| 2 oz. | scotch |
| 2 oz. | white crème de menthe |

Pour ingredients into a mixing glass nearly filled with ice. Stir. Strain into a cocktail glass.

International Stinger

1 oz.	Galliano
1 oz.	white crème de menthe
1 oz.	Metaxa

Pour ingredients into a mixing glass nearly filled with ice. Stir. Strain into a cocktail glass.

Amaretto Stinger

| 2 oz. | Amaretto |
| 2 oz. | white crème de menthe |

Pour ingredients into a mixing glass nearly filled with ice. Stir. Strain into a cocktail glass.

Bee Stinger

| ¹/₂ oz. | white crème de menthe |
| 1¹/₂ oz. | blackberry brandy |

Pour ingredients into a mixing glass nearly filled with ice. Stir. Strain into a cocktail glass.

Grasshopper

1 oz.	green crème de menthe
1 oz.	white crème de cacao
1 oz.	light cream

Combine all ingredients in a shaker nearly filled with ice. Shake well. Strain into a cocktail glass.

Flying Grasshopper

1 oz.	green crème de menthe
1 oz.	white crème de cacao
1 oz.	vodka

Combine all ingredients in a shaker nearly filled with ice. Shake well. Strain into a cocktail glass.

Silver Spider Shooter

¹/₂ oz.	vodka
¹/₂ oz.	rum
¹/₂ oz.	Triple Sec
¹/₂ oz.	white crème de menthe

Pour ingredients into a mixing glass nearly filled with ice. Stir. Strain into a shot glass.

Scorpion

2 oz.	light rum
¹/₂ oz.	brandy
1 oz.	lemon juice
2 oz.	orange juice
¹/₂ oz.	orgeat (almond) syrup

Combine all ingredients in a blender in this order: rum, brandy, orgeat, juices, and ice. Blend thoroughly. Pour into a highball or collins glass. Serve with a fruit slice and a straw.

Tarantula

1½ oz.   scotch
1 oz.   sweet vermouth
½ oz.   Benedictine

Pour ingredients into a mixing glass nearly filled with ice. Stir. Strain into a cocktail glass. Garnish with a lemon twist.

Yellowjacket (Non-alcoholic)

2 oz.   pineapple juice
2 oz.   orange juice
½ oz.   lemon juice

Combine all ingredients in a shaker nearly filled with ice. Shake well. Strain into an old-fashioned glass filled with ice. Garnish with a lemon slice.

THE PERFECT MARTINI

The perfect Martini is the Holy Grail of mixed drinks. The cocktail's origins are obscure, its history debatable, and its preparation endlessly controversial. Given that gin and vermouth are the only two ingredients, it may be hard to grasp the dispute, but not to Martini aficionados. Decades-long debates survive about the preparation and the proportion of gin to vermouth, which ranges from 1 part vermouth to anywhere between 5 and 15 parts gin. Obviously, the less vermouth, the drier the drink, and it is this chilled, crisp dryness that makes the ultimate Martini.

The Martini is presented with a cocktail olive, a pitted green olive without pimento, or a twist of lemon peel. Served with a cocktail onion, the drink is called a Gibson. Today, the Vodka Martini has supplanted its elegant predecessor, but the quest for the perfect drink continues. The mystique of the Martini wouldn't be the same without it.

Martini

Since a Martini is so personal, it is tempting to offer the simplest recipe of 3 ounces gin and vermouth to taste. The following have exact proportions with which to begin an individual Martini odyssey.

2$\frac{1}{2}$ oz. gin
$\frac{1}{2}$ oz. dry vermouth

In a mixing glass half filled with ice, add the vermouth first, then the gin. Stir. Strain into a cocktail glass. Serve with one or two olives or a twist of lemon.

Martini Dry

3 oz. gin
splash dry vermouth

In a mixing glass half filled with ice, add the vermouth first, then the gin. Stir. Strain into a cocktail glass. Serve with one or two olives or a twist of lemon.

James Bond Martini

3 oz. gin
1 oz. vodka
$\frac{1}{2}$ oz. Lillet
     lemon peel

Combine ingredients in a shaker with ice. Shake. Strain into a cocktail glass. Add a slice of lemon peel.

Gibson

2$\frac{1}{2}$ oz. gin
$\frac{1}{2}$ oz. dry vermouth

In a mixing glass half filled with ice, add the vermouth first, then the gin. Stir. Strain into a cocktail glass. Serve with cocktail onions.

Vodka Martini

2$\frac{1}{2}$ oz. vodka
$\frac{1}{2}$ oz. dry vermouth

In a mixing glass half filled with ice, add the vermouth first, then the gin. Stir. Strain into a cocktail glass. Serve with one or two olives or a twist of lemon. For a drier drink, reduce the vermouth.

Lemon Vodka Martini

2 oz. lemon vodka
3 drops Cointreau

Combine ingredients in a shaker with ice. Shake. Strain into a cocktail glass. Serve with a twist of lemon.

Tequila Martini

2$\frac{1}{2}$ oz. tequila
$\frac{1}{2}$ oz. dry vermouth

In a mixing glass half filled with ice, add the vermouth first, then the gin. Stir. Strain into a cocktail glass. Serve with an olive and a twist of lemon.

I'LL TAKE MANHATTAN

The Manhattan, rival to the Martini, is a classy drink in its own right. It's named, aptly, after the Manhattan Club where it was invented and perhaps first served at a gubernatorial celebration in 1894. Unlike garrulous Martini drinkers, fans of the Manhattan allow for both sweet and dry versions. A Manhattan retains its name even if rum, tequila, or Southern Comfort is substituted for whiskey.

Manhattan

2 oz.	blended whiskey
3/4 oz.	sweet vermouth
dash	bitters
	maraschino cherry

Combine whiskey, vermouth, and bitters in a mixing glass half filled with ice. Stir and then strain into a cocktail glass. Garnish with a cherry.

Dry Manhattan

2 oz.	blended whiskey
3/4 oz.	dry vermouth
dash	bitters
	maraschino cherry

Note the change from sweet to dry vermouth. In a mixing glass half filled with ice, stir and then strain into a cocktail glass. Garnish with a cherry.

Perfect Manhattan

2 1/2 oz.	blended whiskey
1/2 oz.	dry vermouth
1/2 oz.	sweet vermouth
dash	bitters
	maraschino cherry

Combine whiskey, vermouths, and bitters in a mixing glass half filled with ice. Stir and then strain into a cocktail glass. Garnish with a cherry.

Rob Roy

2 oz.	scotch
3/4 oz.	sweet vermouth
	maraschino cherry

Combine scotch and vermouth in a mixing glass half filled with ice. Stir and then strain into a cocktail glass. Garnish with a cherry.

Tequila Manhattan

2 oz.   tequila
¾ oz.   sweet vermouth
          maraschino cherry

Combine tequila and vermouth in a mixing glass half filled with ice. Stir and then strain into a cocktail glass. Garnish with a cherry.

Comfort Manhattan

2 oz.   Southern Comfort
¾ oz.   sweet vermouth
          maraschino cherry

Combine Southern Comfort and vermouth in a mixing glass half filled with ice. Stir and then strain into a cocktail glass. Garnish with a cherry.

Latin Manhattan

1 oz.   rum
1 oz.   dry vermouth
1 oz.   sweet vermouth
          maraschino cherry

Pour ingredients into a mixing glass nearly filled with ice. Stir. Strain into a cocktail glass. Garnish with a cherry.

Mock Manhattan (non-alcoholic)

2 oz.   orange juice
2 oz.   cranberry juice
splash   lemon juice
splash   maraschino cherry
          juice
dash   orange bitters
          maraschino cherry

Pour ingredients into a mixing glass nearly filled with ice. Stir. Strain into a cocktail glass. Garnish with a cherry.

• •

Mixing Your Own Non-Alcoholic Drinks
The Beauty is in the Balance

• •

Mixing a satisfying drink without alcohol is not like pouring a glass of juice in the morning. A drink that is sparkling or spicy, mellow or refreshing, requires a careful consideration of ingredients. Your first thought should be of a flavor that delights you. The rest is a question of balance. Every recipe should be a blend of at least two of the following flavor elements:

- *A basic flavor:* Either sweet/acid, like orange juice; acid/sweet, like pineapple juice; or just plain acid, like tomato juice.
- *A neutral flavor:* An extender, either unflavored, like club soda, or naturally flavored, like ginger ale. If you crave a drink with intense flavor, an extender may be unnecessary.
- *A balance flavor:* An accent flavor that enhances or offsets the basic flavor. With a sweet basic flavor, use an acid balance, and vice versa.

Here is a recipe for real ginger ale that allows you to get very personal with your drink. You can adjust the proportions to make it just the way you like it.

Real Ginger Ale
Basic flavor: ginger syrup (sweet)
Neutral flavor: club soda
Balance flavor: lime juice (acid)

• •

HOT STUFF: THE BLOODY MARY

A bartender at Harry's New York Bar in Paris in the 1920s is credited with creating the Bloody Mary. It was then called the Red Snapper, and rightly so, because a Bloody Mary should quiver your taste buds with a snap and fire up your tongue. Preference and Tabasco dictate the amount of flame in this drink, but a Bloody Mary deserving of its name should never be a Plain Jane.

Tequila Maria

2 oz.	tequila
4 oz.	tomato juice
splash	lemon juice
dash	Worcestershire sauce
dash	Tabasco sauce
shake	salt & pepper

Pour all ingredients into a highball glass over ice and stir well. Garnish with a lime wedge.

Bloody Caesar Shooter

1	littleneck clam
1 oz.	vodka
1½ oz.	tomato juice
dash	Worcestershire sauce
dash	Tabasco
dash	horseradish

Place a clam in the bottom of a shot glass. Add all other ingredients. Stir.

Bloody Mary

2 oz.	vodka
4 oz.	tomato juice
1/2 oz.	lemon juice
dash	Worcestershire sauce
dash	Tabasco sauce
shake	salt & pepper
shake	celery salt

Pour all ingredients into a highball glass over ice and stir well. Garnish with a celery stick and lime wedge.

Virgin Mary
(Non-alcoholic)

6 oz.	V-8 juice
1/2 oz.	lemon juice
dash	Worcestershire sauce
dash	Tabasco sauce
1/4 tsp.	horseradish

Pour all ingredients into a highball glass over ice and stir well. Garnish with a celery stick.

Clamato Cocktail

2 oz.	vodka
3 oz.	tomato juice
2 oz.	clam juice
dash	Worcestershire sauce
dash	Tabasco sauce

Pour all ingredients into a highball glass over ice and stir well. Garnish with a lemon wedge.

Hot Clamato
(Non-alcoholic)

6 oz.	Clamato juice
1 oz.	lime juice or juice of 1/2 lime
dash	Worcestershire sauce
dash	Tabasco sauce
1/4 tsp.	horseradish

Pour all ingredients into a highball glass over ice and stir well. Garnish with a lemon wedge.

Bloody Bull

2 oz.	vodka
3 oz.	tomato juice
2 oz.	beef bouillon
dash	Worcestershire sauce
dash	Tabasco sauce

Pour all ingredients into a highball glass over ice and stir well. Garnish with a lime wedge.

Slumbering Bull
(Non-alcoholic)

5 oz.	V-8 juice
2 oz.	beef bouillon
dash	Tabasco
dash	Worcestershire sauce
dash	celery salt

Pour all ingredients into a highball glass over ice and stir well. Garnish with a lime wedge.

COMING UP DAISIES

The flower power in a Daisy is luscious
grenadine, a syrup made from pomegranates.
Gin, brandy, rum, scotch, whiskey, and vodka
bloom as Daisies, so you can grow your own.

Whiskey Daisy

2 oz.	blended whiskey
1 oz.	lemon juice or juice of ½ lemon
½ tsp.	fine sugar
1 tsp.	grenadine

Combine the liquor, lemon juice, sugar, and grenadine in a shaker half filled with ice. Shake well. Pour into an old-fashioned glass. Garnish with a cherry and fruit.

Rum Daisy

2 oz.	rum
1 oz.	lemon juice or juice of ½ lemon
½ tsp.	fine sugar
1 tsp.	grenadine

Combine the liquor, lemon juice, sugar, and grenadine in a shaker half filled with ice. Shake well. Pour into an old-fashioned glass. Garnish with a cherry and fruit.

Vodka Daisy

2 oz.	vodka
1 oz.	lemon juice or juice of ½ lemon
½ tsp.	fine sugar
1 tsp.	grenadine

Combine the liquor, lemon juice, sugar, and grenadine in a shaker half filled with ice. Shake well. Pour into an old-fashioned glass. Garnish with a cherry and fruit.

Gin Daisy

2 oz.	gin
1 oz.	lemon juice or juice of ½ lemon
½ tsp.	fine sugar
1 tsp.	grenadine

Combine the liquor, lemon juice, sugar, and grenadine in a shaker half filled with ice. Shake well. Pour into an old-fashioned glass. Garnish with a cherry and fruit.

Brandy Daisy

2 oz.	brandy
1 oz.	lemon juice or juice of 1/2 lemon
1/2 tsp.	fine sugar
1 tsp.	grenadine

Combine the liquor, lemon juice, sugar, and grenadine in a shaker half filled with ice. Shake well. Pour into an old-fashioned glass. Garnish with a cherry and fruit.

Scotch Daisy

2 oz.	scotch
1 oz.	lemon juice or juice of 1/2 lemon
1/2 tsp.	fine sugar
1 tsp.	grenadine

Combine the liquor, lemon juice, sugar, and grenadine in a shaker half filled with ice. Shake well. Pour into an old-fashioned glass. Garnish with a cherry and fruit.

Lemon Daisy (Non-alcoholic)

2 oz.	lemon juice or juice of 1 lemon
1 oz.	grenadine
1 oz.	lemon and lime soda
1 oz.	sparkling water

Pour lemon juice and grenadine over ice in an old-fashioned glass. Stir well. Add equal parts lemon and lime soda and sparkling water. Stir gently. Add a lemon twist.

PART IV
CRAZY NAMES

Drinks to Travel By, The Russians Are
Coming, Drinks à la Française, Sweet
as a Kiss, Sex Drinks, Raise Your
Glass to the Weather, The Heavens,
Royalty at the Bar, Namesakes,
Zombies and Other Horrors,
A Menagerie in a Glass

DRINKS TO TRAVEL BY

Have a "New Orleans" cocktail and think Mardi Gras. Try a "Palm Beach" and listen to the ocean. Sip a "San Francisco" and view the Golden Gate. "Woodstock!" Take out that tie-dyed shirt. People have always gone armchair traveling with drinks in hand. Casablanca is a favorite. You could meet Humphrey Bogart there.

Palm Beach

1½ oz.	gin
1 tsp.	sweet vermouth
2 oz.	grapefruit juice

Combine ingredients in a shaker half filled with ice. Shake well. Strain into a cocktail glass.

San Francisco

1 oz.	sloe gin
¾ oz.	sweet vermouth
¾ oz.	dry vermouth
dash	bitters
dash	orange bitters

Combine ingredients in a shaker half filled with ice. Shake well. Strain into a cocktail glass.

New Orleans

2 oz.	bourbon
½ oz.	Pernod
dash	Anisette
dash	bitters
dash	orange bitters
1 tsp.	fine sugar

Combine ingredients in a shaker half filled with ice. Shake well. Strain into an old-fashioned glass over ice. Serve with a lemon twist.

Saratoga

2 oz.	brandy
½ tsp.	Maraschino
1 tsp.	lemon juice
1 Tbs.	pineapple juice
dash	bitters

Combine ingredients in a shaker half filled with ice. Shake well. Strain into a cocktail glass.

Woodstock

1½ oz.	gin
1 oz.	lemon juice or juice of ½ lemon
1 Tbs.	maple syrup
dash	orange bitters

Combine ingredients in a shaker half filled with ice. Shake well. Strain into a cocktail glass.

Sevilla

1½ oz.	light rum
1½ oz.	tawny port
1 tsp.	fine sugar
1	egg

Combine ingredients in a shaker half filled with ice. Shake well. Strain into a wine glass.

Miami Beach

1½ oz.	scotch
1 oz.	dry vermouth
1½ oz.	grapefruit juice

Combine ingredients in a shaker half filled with ice. Shake well. Strain into an old-fashioned glass over ice.

San Juan Capistrano
(Non-alcoholic)

2 oz.	grapefruit juice
2 oz.	coconut cream
1 oz.	lime juice or juice of ½ lime

Combine ingredients in a blender with ice. Blend thoroughly. Pour into a large wine glass.

Glasgow

2 oz.	scotch
1 tsp.	dry vermouth
1 tsp.	lemon juice
1 tsp.	almond extract

Combine ingredients in a shaker half filled with ice. Shake well. Strain into an old-fashioned glass.

Casablanca

2 oz.	light rum
½ oz.	Cointreau
½ oz.	Maraschino
½ oz.	lime juice

Combine ingredients in a shaker half filled with ice. Shake well. Strain into a cocktail glass.

Nevada Cocktail

1½ oz.	light rum
1½ oz.	grapefruit juice
1 oz.	lime juice or juice of ½ lime
3 tsp.	fine sugar
dash	bitters

Combine ingredients in a shaker nearly filled with ice. Strain into a cocktail glass.

New York

1½ oz.	blended whiskey
1 oz.	lemon juice or juice of ½ lemon
1 tsp.	fine sugar
½ tsp.	grenadine

Combine ingredients in a shaker half filled with ice. Shake well. Strain into a cocktail glass. Serve with a lemon twist.

Florida

1 oz.	gin
1 tsp.	Kirschwasser
1 tsp.	Cointreau
1 oz.	orange juice
1 tsp.	lemon juice

Combine ingredients in a shaker half filled with ice. Shake well. Strain into a cocktail glass.

Sunshine State (Non-alcoholic)

4 oz.	cherry soda
1/2 cup	orange sherbet
1 tsp.	lemon juice

Combine ingredients in a blender with ice. Blend well. Pour into a collins or highball glass. Serve with a straw.

Montana

2 oz.	brandy
1 1/2 oz.	port
1/2 oz.	dry vermouth

Pour ingredients into an old-fashioned glass over ice. Stir.

Alaska

2 oz.	gin
3/4 oz.	yellow Chartreuse
2 dashes	orange bitters

Combine ingredients in a shaker half filled with ice. Shake well. Strain into a cocktail glass.

Kentucky

| 2 oz. | bourbon |
| 1 oz. | pineapple juice |

Combine ingredients in a shaker half filled with ice. Shake well. Strain into a cocktail glass.

Washington

2 oz.	dry vermouth
1 oz.	brandy
1 tsp.	fine sugar
dash	bitters

Combine ingredients in a shaker half filled with ice. Shake well. Strain into a cocktail glass.

Louisville Cooler

1½ oz.	bourbon
1 oz.	orange juice
1 Tbs.	lime juice
1 tsp.	fine sugar

Combine ingredients in a shaker half filled with ice. Strain into an old-fashioned glass filled with ice. Garnish with an orange slice.

Kentucky Blizzard

1½ oz.	bourbon
1½ oz.	cranberry juice
½ oz.	lime juice
½ oz.	grenadine
1 tsp.	fine sugar

Combine ingredients in a shaker half filled with ice. Strain into an old-fashioned glass filled with ice. Garnish with an orange slice.

Brooklyn

2 oz.	rye whiskey
1 oz.	dry vermouth
dash	Amer Picon
dash	Maraschino

Combine ingredients in a shaker half filled with ice. Shake well. Strain into a cocktail glass.

Quebec

1½ oz.	Canadian whiskey
½ oz.	dry vermouth
1½ tsp.	Amer Picon
1½ tsp.	Maraschino

Combine ingredients in a shaker half filled with ice. Shake well. Strain into a cocktail glass.

Long Island Iced Tea

½ oz.	tequila
½ oz.	gin
½ oz.	light rum
½ oz.	vodka
1 oz.	lemon juice or juice of ½ lemon
1 tsp.	fine sugar
	cola

Combine all ingredients except cola in a shaker half filled with ice. Shake well. Strain into a highball glass over ice. Top with cola. Stir.

Narragansett

2 oz.	bourbon
1 oz.	sweet vermouth
dash	anisette

Pour ingredients into an old-fashioned glass nearly filled with ice. Stir. Add a lemon twist.

La Jolla

1½ oz.	brandy
½ oz.	crème de banane
2 tsp.	orange juice
1 tsp.	lemon juice

Combine ingredients in a shaker nearly filled with ice. Strain into a cocktail glass.

La Hoya (Non-alcoholic)

2 slices	banana
2 oz.	orange juice
1 oz.	grapefruit juice
1 tsp.	lemon juice

Combine ingredients in a blender without ice. Blend thoroughly. Pour into a cocktail glass.

THE RUSSIANS ARE COMING

If a drink has "Russian" in the title, vodka is its inspiration. Most "Russian" drinks take their cue from the popular "Black Russian," vodka and coffee liqueur. They are pared down, no-nonsense drinks with a single, to-the-point taste. These drinks may be coffee or mocha or strawberry, but they are elevated from the prosaic by the presence of vodka, which may be tasteless, but never, never pointless.

White Russian

1½ oz.	vodka
½ oz.	coffee liqueur
½ oz.	cream

Combine ingredients in a shaker half filled with ice. Shake well. Strain into an old-fashioned glass over ice.

Black Russian

1½ oz.	vodka
½ oz.	coffee liqueur

Pour vodka and liqueur into an old-fashioned glass nearly filled with ice. Stir well.

Russian Kamikaze Shooter

2 oz.	vodka
1 tsp.	Chambord

Pour ingredients into a mixing glass nearly filled with ice. Stir. Strain into a shot glass.

Russian Cocktail

1 oz.	vodka
½ oz.	gin
½ oz.	white crème de cacao

Pour ingredients into a mixing glass nearly filled with ice. Stir. Strain into a cocktail glass.

Red Russian

1 oz.   strawberry liqueur
1 oz.   vodka
½ oz.   cream

Combine ingredients in a shaker half filled with ice. Shake well. Strain into an old-fashioned glass over ice.

Creamy Red Russian (Non-alcoholic)

¼ cup   strawberries, fresh or frozen
1 Tbs.   fine sugar
1 oz.   cream

Combine ingredients in a blender with 1 cup of ice. Blend thoroughly. Pour into a large red wine glass. Serve with a straw.

Russian Coffee

½ oz.   vodka
½ oz.   coffee liqueur
½ oz.   hazelnut liqueur
4 oz.   hot coffee
          whipped cream or cream

Pour vodka and liqueurs into an Irish Coffee glass or mug. Stir. Add coffee. Stir. Top with whipped cream or cream poured over the back of a spoon so it will float on top.

Russian Bear

1 oz.   vodka
1 oz.   dark crème de cacao
½ oz.   cream

Combine ingredients in a shaker half filled with ice. Shake well. Strain into an old-fashioned glass over ice.

Chocolate Black Russian

1 oz.   coffee liqueur
1 oz.   vodka
2 scoops chocolate ice cream

Combine ingredients in a blender without ice. Blend thoroughly. Pour into a large red wine glass. To make drink thicker, add crushed ice to blender.

Frozen Mocha Russian (Non-alcoholic)

2 oz.   cold black coffee
2 scoops chocolate ice cream

Combine ingredients in a blender without ice. Blend thoroughly. Pour into a large red wine glass. Top with chocolate shavings.

À LA FRANÇAISE

The French have a certain style that Americans find, well, seductive.

And drinks with a French connection are often alluring. Some remind us of Paris's most provocative places. "Moulin Rouge" brings to mind the nightclub made famous by Toulouse-Lautrec's paintings. "Montmartre" recalls the hilltop enclave of artists that crowns the city. "Champs Elysées" marks Europe's most famous promenade. Perhaps an infatuated American coined these drink names. The French, after all, are more interested in wine.

French Connection

| 2 oz. | cognac |
| 1½ oz. | Amaretto |

Combine ingredients in a shaker half filled with ice. Shake well. Strain into a cocktail glass.

Moulin Rouge

1½ oz.	sloe gin
½ oz.	sweet vermouth
dash	bitters

Pour ingredients into a mixing glass nearly filled with ice. Stir. Strain into a cocktail glass.

Montmartre

1½ oz.	gin
½ oz.	sweet vermouth
½ oz.	Cointreau

Combine ingredients in a shaker half filled with ice. Shake well. Strain into a cocktail glass.

Parisian

1½ oz.	gin
1 oz.	dry vermouth
½ oz.	crème de cassis

Combine ingredients in a shaker half filled with ice. Shake well. Strain into a cocktail glass.

French Cream Punch

1 cup	Amaretto
1 cup	coffee liqueur or coffee brandy
¼ cup	Triple Sec
½ gallon	softened vanilla ice cream

Mix well and do not add ice. Makes 15-20 servings.

Champs Elysées

1½ oz.	brandy
½ oz.	sweet vermouth
½ oz.	lemon juice
½ oz.	fine sugar
dash	bitters

Combine ingredients in a shaker half filled with ice. Shake well. Strain into a cocktail glass.

French "75"

2 oz.	gin
1½ oz.	lemon juice or juice of 1 lemon
2 tsp.	fine sugar
2 oz.	chilled champagne

Combine ingredients except champagne in a shaker half filled with ice. Shake well. Strain into a highball glass. Add champagne. Stir gently. Garnish with a fruit slice and cherry.

French Breeze

| 2 oz. | Pernod |
| 1 oz. | peppermint schnapps |

Combine ingredients in a shaker half filled with ice. Shake well. Strain into a cocktail glass.

Parisian Blonde Shooter

½ oz.	light rum
½ oz.	Triple Sec
½ oz.	dark rum

Combine ingredients in a shaker half filled with ice. Shake well. Strain into a shot glass.

AS SWEET AS A KISS

Kissing is an art and a passion and the most natural act in the world. Kiss your parents, your children, your friends, and you express affection. Kiss your lover and affection escalates to "Kiss in the Dark" and "Soul Kiss," drinks that call up deep desires. Good as these drinks may be, there are some thirsts they just cannot quench.

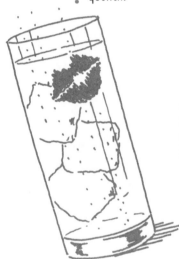

Kiss Me Quick

1½ oz.	Pernod
½ tsp.	Curaçao
3 dashes	bitters
	club soda

Combine Pernod, Curaçao, and bitters in a shaker half filled with ice. Shake well. Pour into a highball glass with ice. Add club soda and stir gently.

Velvet Kiss

1½ oz.	gin
½ oz.	crème de banane
1 oz.	pineapple juice
½ oz.	light cream

Combine ingredients in a shaker half filled with ice. Shake well. Strain into a cocktail glass.

Kiss on the Lips

1½ oz.	bourbon
5 oz.	apricot nectar

Pour into a collins glass nearly filled with ice. Stir gently. Serve with a straw.

Kiss on the Cheek (Non-alcoholic)

2 oz.	apricot nectar
1 oz.	lemon juice or juice of ½ lemon
	club soda

Pour apricot nectar and lemon juice into a mixing glass nearly filled with ice. Stir well. Strain into a highball glass over ice. Garnish with a lemon twist.

Kiss in the Dark

1 oz.	gin
½ oz.	cherry brandy
½ oz.	dry vermouth

Pour ingredients into a mixing glass nearly filled with ice. Stir. Strain into a cocktail glass.

Kiss the Boys Good-bye

1½ oz.	brandy
½ oz.	sloe gin
1 oz.	lemon juice or juice of ½ lemon
1	egg white

Combine ingredients in a shaker half filled with ice. Shake well. Strain into a cocktail glass.

Soul Kiss

1 oz.	bourbon
½ oz.	dry vermouth
½ oz.	Dubonnet rouge
½ oz.	orange juice

Combine ingredients in a shaker half filled with ice. Shake well. Strain into a cocktail glass.

Sonny Gets Kissed

1½ oz.	light rum
½ oz.	apricot brandy
1 tsp.	lime juice
1 tsp.	lemon juice
½ tsp.	fine sugar

Combine ingredients in a shaker half filled with ice. Shake well. Strain into a cocktail glass.

SEX DRINKS

When did sex move out of the bedroom and into the bar? Honey, where have you been? Sexiness and drinking establishments have coexisted quite nicely, thank you, since men wore cravats and the exposure of a woman's ankle was considered risqué. Today, a woman can walk up to a bartender and ask for a "Screaming Orgasm." And all she'll get is a drink.

Between the Sheets

½ oz.	light rum
½ oz.	brandy
½ oz.	lemon juice
½ oz.	Curaçao

Combine ingredients in a shaker half filled with ice. Shake well. Strain into a cocktail glass.

Bosom Caresser

1½ oz.	brandy
1 oz.	Madeira
½ oz.	Triple Sec

Pour ingredients into a mixing glass nearly filled with ice. Stir. Strain into a cocktail glass.

Menage à Trois

1 oz.	light rum
1 oz.	Cointreau
1 oz.	light cream

Combine ingredients in a shaker half filled with ice. Shake well. Strain into a cocktail glass.

Sex on the Beach

1½ oz.	vodka
1 oz.	peach-flavored brandy
2 oz.	orange juice
2 oz.	cranberry juice

Combine all ingredients in a highball glass almost filled with ice. Stir.

Safe Sex on the Beach (Non-alcoholic)

2 oz.	peach nectar
3 oz.	cranberry juice
3 oz.	orange juice

Combine all ingredients in a highball or collins glass nearly filled with ice. Stir. Garnish with a cherry.

Sleazy Sex on the Beach

1½ oz.	vodka
1 oz.	Grand Marnier
2 oz.	orange juice
2 oz.	cranberry juice

Combine all ingredients in a highball glass almost filled with ice. Stir.

Slippery Nipple

2 oz.	Sambuca
1 oz.	Irish cream liqueur
dash	grenadine

Pour Sambuca into a cocktail glass. Carefully float liqueur on top. Drop grenadine in the center of the drink.

Hot Pants

1½ oz.	tequila
½ oz.	peppermint schnapps
½ oz.	grapefruit juice
1 tsp.	fine sugar

Combine ingredients in a shaker half filled with ice. Shake well. Strain into an old-fashioned glass with salt.

Orgasm

1½ oz.	vodka
1½ oz.	Triple Sec
splash	lime juice
½ tsp.	fine sugar
	club soda or 7-Up

In a highball glass, dissolve sugar in lime juice. Nearly fill glass with ice. Add liquor and soda. Stir.

Screaming Orgasm

½ oz.	Grand Marnier
½ oz.	Irish cream liqueur
½ oz.	coffee liqueur

Combine ingredients in a shaker half filled with ice. Shake well. Strain into a shot glass.

Dirty Girl Scout

1 oz.	vodka
1 oz.	coffee liqueur
1 oz.	Irish cream liqueur
1 tsp.	green crème de menthe

Combine ingredients in a shaker half filled with ice. Shake well. Strain into an old-fashioned glass with ice.

Quiet Passion (Non-alcoholic)

3 oz.	white grape juice
3 oz.	grapefruit juice
1 oz.	passion fruit juice

Combine ingredients in a shaker half filled with ice. Shake well. Strain into a collins or highball glass over ice.

Affair

1 oz.	strawberry schnapps
1 oz.	cranberry juice
1 oz.	orange juice

Pour ingredients into a mixing glass nearly filled with ice. Stir. Strain into a cocktail glass.

Maiden No More

1½ oz.	gin
½ oz.	Cointreau
1 Tbs.	brandy
1 tsp.	fine sugar
1 oz.	lemon juice or juice of ½ lemon

Combine ingredients in a shaker half filled with ice. Shake well. Strain into a cocktail glass.

Blowjob

½ oz.	vodka
½ oz.	coffee brandy
½ oz.	coffee liqueur

Combine ingredients in a shaker half filled with ice. Shake well. Strain into a shot glass.

RAISE YOUR GLASS TO THE WEATHER

Weather elates us, depresses us, makes or breaks our days. Why not pick a drink to match the weather: join forces with "Dark and Stormy," snuggle up with "Foggy Afternoon," raise your glass to "Damn the Weather," and let the elements be hanged.

Dark and Stormy

1½ oz.	dark rum
4 oz.	ginger beer
	lime wedge

Pour rum into a highball glass nearly filled with ice. Add ginger beer. Stir gently. Squeeze a lime wedge over the drink.

Fair and Warmer

1½ oz.	light rum
½ oz.	sweet vermouth
splash	Curaçao

Combine ingredients in a shaker half filled with ice. Shake well. Strain into a cocktail glass. Add a lemon twist.

Heat Wave

1½ oz.	light rum
½ oz.	peach-flavored brandy
½ oz.	coconut cream
2 oz.	orange juice
2 oz.	pineapple juice
½ oz.	grenadine

Pour all ingredients except grenadine into a highball or parfait glass over ice. Stir well. Top with grenadine. Garnish with a fruit slice.

Hurricane

1 oz.	light rum
1 oz.	dark rum
2 Tbs.	passion fruit syrup
1 tsp.	lime juice

Combine ingredients in a shaker half filled with ice. Shake well. Strain into a cocktail glass.

Eye of the Hurricane (Non-alcoholic)

2 oz.	passion fruit syrup
1 oz.	lime juice or juice of ½ lime
	club soda or lemon & lime soda

Combine syrup and lime juice in a mixing glass nearly filled with ice. Strain into a highball or collins glass over ice. Add soda. Garnish with a wedge of lime.

Gale at Sea

1½ oz.	vodka
½ oz.	dry vermouth
½ oz.	Galliano
½ oz.	blue Curaçao

Pour ingredients into a mixing glass nearly filled with ice. Stir. Strain into a cocktail glass.

Foggy Afternoon

1 oz.	vodka
1/2 oz.	apricot brandy
1/2 oz.	Triple Sec
1 tsp.	crème de banane
1 tsp.	lemon juice

Combine ingredients in a shaker half filled with ice. Shake well. Strain into a cocktail glass.

Hazy Day (Non-alcoholic)

3 slices	banana
1 oz.	apricot nectar
1 oz.	orange juice
1 tsp.	lemon juice

Mash banana slices. Combine with other ingredients in a shaker half filled with ice. Shake well. Strain into a cocktail glass.

Damn the Weather

1 1/2 oz.	gin
1 Tbs.	sweet vermouth
1 Tbs.	Cointreau
1 oz.	orange juice

Combine ingredients in a shaker half filled with ice. Shake well. Strain into a cocktail glass.

Thunderclap

1 1/2 oz.	whiskey
1/2 oz.	gin
1/2 oz.	brandy

Pour ingredients into a mixing glass nearly filled with ice. Stir. Strain into a cocktail glass.

Blizzard

2 oz.	bourbon
2 oz.	cranberry juice
1/2 oz.	lemon juice
1 tsp.	fine sugar

Combine bourbon, sugar, juices, and ice in a blender in that order. Blend well. Pour into a collins or highball glass. Serve with a straw.

Tropical Rainstorm

1 1/2 oz.	dark rum
1 tsp.	Triple Sec
1/2 oz.	cherry brandy
1/2 oz.	lemon juice

Combine ingredients in a shaker half filled with ice. Shake well. Strain into a cocktail glass.

Party Time Prep

Planning ahead really does ensure the spontaneity of your party. And nothing ruins a good time like running out of the bare necessities. Quantities all depend on how many guests are invited, the particular occasion, and when the party is called for.

The standard cocktail party usually lasts four hours. Use this list as a shopping guide before the guests arrive:

- *Ice.* If you run out, there's no substitute. So be prepared with about one pound per person.

- *Liquor.* One liter for every six guests. Choose at least two kinds of light alcohol, like gin or vodka, and two dark, like scotch or bourbon.

- *Wine.* White and red. One case (twelve bottles) contains about sixty servings.

- *Beer.* One case (twenty-four bottles) serves every ten guests. However, if beer is the beverage of choice for your crowd, one case might only serve six guests.

- *Vermouth.* Sweet and dry. You never know who might drop by.

- *Mixers.* For every liter of liquor, you'll need about two quarts of mixers. Tonic water, club soda, fruit juices, and cola are must-haves. Lemon and lime soda, tomato, cranberry, grapefruit, pineapple, and orange juices will also work well as simple non-alcoholic drinks.

- *Garnishes.* Lemons and limes. For wedges and slices, assume one lemon for every twenty people, and one lime for every five.

- *Napkins.* You'll need plenty for both your guests and your furniture.

THE HEAVENS

Sunrise, sunset, moonlight, and stars—these are the heaven-sent gifts that we often miss. We're either too late, too early, too busy, or too tired. These are our excuses. Luckily, we have "Tequila Sunrise" and "Caribbean Sunset," "Moonlight," and even a drink named "Golden Dawn." Any time at all, they offer us a little bit of heaven.

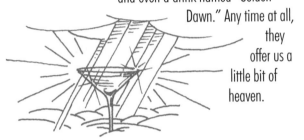

Star

| 1½ oz. | applejack |
| 1½ oz. | sweet vermouth |

Combine ingredients in a shaker half filled with ice. Shake well. Strain into a cocktail glass.

Moonlight

2 oz.	apple brandy
2 oz.	lemon juice
1 tsp.	fine sugar

Combine ingredients in a shaker half filled with ice. Shake well. Strain into an old-fashioned glass over ice.

Caribbean Sunset

4 oz.	red wine
2 tsp.	Cointreau
dash	orange bitters
	club soda

Combine ingredients in a large wine glass. Stir well. Add a lemon twist.

Venetian Sunset

1½ oz.	Grappa
3 oz.	orange juice
2 dashes	Campari

Combine ingredients in a shaker half filled with ice. Shake well. Strain into a cocktail glass.

Red Apple Sunset
(Non-alcoholic)

3 oz.	apple juice
1 oz.	grapefruit juice
4 dashes	grenadine

Combine ingredients in a shaker half filled with ice. Shake well. Strain into a cocktail glass.

Eclipse

1½ oz.	sloe gin
1 oz.	gin
1 tsp.	grenadine
	maraschino cherry

Place the maraschino cherry in a cocktail glass. Cover with grenadine (more than a tsp. may be required). Combine gins in a shaker half filled with ice. Shake well. Strain carefully into the glass so that the grenadine is not disturbed. Garnish with an orange twist.

Golden Dawn

1½ oz.	gin
1 oz.	apricot liqueur
1 oz.	lime juice or juice of ½ lime
1 oz.	orange juice
dash	grenadine

Combine ingredients in a shaker half filled with ice. Shake well. Strain into a cocktail glass.

Rosy Dawn
(Non-alcoholic)

1 oz.	lemon juice or juice of ½ lemon
1 oz.	lime juice or juice of ½ lime
2 oz.	orange juice
1 oz.	coconut cream
1 tsp.	grenadine
1 tsp.	orgeat (almond) syrup

Combine ingredients in a blender with ice. Blend thoroughly. Pour into a large wine glass.

Tequila Sunrise

2 oz.	tequila
4 oz.	orange juice
¾ oz.	grenadine

Pour tequila and orange juice into a highball glass over ice. Stir well. Pour in grenadine slowly so it floats on top.

Cape Cod Sunrise
(Non-alcoholic)

3 oz.	cranberry juice
1 oz.	lime juice or juice of ½ lime

Combine ingredients in a shaker half filled with ice. Shake well. Strain into a wine glass over ice. Garnish with a slice of lime.

ROYALTY AT THE BAR

Kings and queens, princes and princesses, even a queen's cousin have drinks named after them. A quick survey reveals that royal recipes have no patterns: no liquor seems more noble than any other. So the link between royal personages and their namesake drinks remains a mystery. History, no doubt has an answer. But no matter. Raising a toast with a "Queen Elizabeth" or a "Prince Edward" is as close as any of us is likely to get to the royals.

Queen Elizabeth

1½ oz.	gin
½ oz.	dry vermouth
1 tsp.	Benedictine

Combine ingredients in a shaker half filled with ice. Shake well. Strain into a cocktail glass.

Duchess

1½ oz.	Pernod
½ oz.	dry vermouth
½ oz.	sweet vermouth

Combine ingredients in a shaker half filled with ice. Shake well. Strain into a cocktail glass.

Prince's Smile

1½ oz.	gin
1 oz.	apple brandy
1 oz.	apricot brandy
1 tsp.	lemon juice

Combine ingredients in a shaker half filled with ice. Shake well. Strain into a cocktail glass.

Little Prince
(Non-alcoholic)

2 oz.	sparkling cider
1 oz.	apricot nectar
1 oz.	lemon juice or juice of ½ lemon

Pour ingredients into a mixing glass nearly filled with ice. Stir. Strain into an old-fashioned glass. Add a lemon twist.

Queen's Cousin

1 oz.	vodka
1 oz.	Grand Marnier
½ oz.	Cointreau
splash	lime juice
dash	bitters
3 oz.	sparkling white wine

Combine ingredients except wine in a shaker half filled with ice. Shake well. Strain into a large wine glass. Add wine and stir.

Little Princess

2 oz.	light rum
1 oz.	sweet vermouth

Combine ingredients in a shaker half filled with ice. Shake well. Strain into a cocktail glass.

Prince Edward

1½ oz.	scotch
½ oz.	Lillet
½ oz.	Drambuie

Combine ingredients in a shaker half filled with ice. Shake well. Strain into an old-fashioned glass. Garnish with an orange slice.

King Kenneth

2 oz.	Campari
1 oz.	peach schnapps
1 oz.	orange juice
1 tsp.	lemon juice
4 oz.	tonic water

Combine all ingredients except tonic in a shaker half filled with ice. Shake well. Strain into a collins or highball glass over ice. Add tonic. Stir. Add a lemon twist.

NAMESAKES

You don't have to be Adam and Eve to have a drink named after you, but they do seem particularly appropriate. "To Life!" is the toast for these two who started it all. Napoleon, a short man who was larger than life, has a dessert and a cocktail bearing his name. Two historically important American figures have drinks named after them, clever Betsy Ross and gallant Robert E. Lee. And three entertainers: the beautiful Mary Pickford, the great Charlie Chaplin, and the wise Will Rogers, who made life his art.

Mary Pickford Cocktail

1 oz.	light rum
1 oz.	pineapple juice
½ tsp.	grenadine
½ tsp.	Maraschino

Combine ingredients in a shaker half filled with ice. Shake well. Strain into a cocktail glass and garnish with a cherry.

Mary's Sister (Non-alcoholic)

| 1 oz. | white grape juice |
| 1 oz. | pineapple juice |

Combine ingredients in a shaker half filled with ice. Shake well. Strain into a cocktail glass and garnish with a cherry.

Adam and Eve

1 oz.	Forbidden Fruit Liqueur
1 oz.	gin
1 oz.	brandy
splash	lemon juice

Pour all ingredients into a shaker half filled with crushed ice. Shake well. Strain into a cocktail glass.

Napoleon

2 oz.	gin
½ oz.	Dubonnet Rouge
½ oz.	Grand Marnier

Stir all ingredients in a mixing glass half filled with ice. Strain into a cocktail glass.

Charlie Chaplin Shooter

1 oz.	sloe gin
1 oz.	apricot-flavored brandy
½ oz.	lemon juice

Combine ingredients in a shaker nearly filled with ice. Shake well. Strain into a shot glass.

Charlie's Cousin (Non-alcoholic)

1 tsp.	frozen orange juice concentrate, thawed
2 oz.	apricot nectar
½ oz.	lemon juice

Combine ingredients in a shaker nearly filled with ice. Shake well. Strain into a shot glass.

Will Rogers

1½ oz.	gin
½ oz.	dry vermouth
1 Tbs..	orange juice
1 dash	Triple Sec

Combine all ingredients in a shaker nearly filled with ice. Shake well. Strain into a cocktail glass.

Cowboy Will's (Non-Alcoholic)

1½ oz.	orange juice
½ oz.	tonic
1 tsp.	fine sugar

Combine all ingredients in a shaker nearly filled with ice. Shake well. Strain into a cocktail glass.

Betsy Ross

2 oz.	brandy
1½ oz.	port
dash	Triple Sec

Combine ingredients in a mixing glass nearly filled with ice. Stir well. Strain into a cocktail glass.

Robert E. Lee Cooler

2 oz.	gin
2 oz.	club soda
¼ tsp.	Anisette
½ tsp.	fine sugar
1 oz.	lime juice or juice of ½ lime
	ginger ale

Combine lime juice, sugar, and club soda in a collins glass. Stir. Add ice cubes, Anisette, and gin. Stir. Fill with ginger ale. Stir well. Garnish with a lemon slice.

Lee's Confederate Cooler (Non-Alcoholic)

2 oz.	white grape juice
2 oz.	club soda
½ tsp.	fine sugar
1 oz.	lime juice or juice of ½ lime
	ginger ale

Combine lime juice, sugar, and club soda in a collins glass. Stir. Add ice cubes, grape juice, and ginger ale. Stir well and serve with a slice of fruit.

Top Ten Party Secrets:

1. Separate the food and drinks. This creates movement or "party flow."
2. Invite guests with different interests—who wants a room full of manicurists or doctors?
3. As the host, try to control your alcohol intake; otherwise, you run the risk of missing out on all the fun.
4. Avoid finger foods that leave something in your hand.
5. Buy top-shelf liquor: your friends are worth it.
6. Theme drinks are a fun idea, but don't count on everyone liking them. Make sure to have enough alternatives, both alcoholic and non-alcoholic.
7. Buy plastic cups rather than paper. All paper cups will eventually drip.
8. Have the makings of a pot of coffee ready.
9. End the party on a high note. Your guests will leave while they are having a good time, and they'll remember it as a successful party.
10. Clean up immediately after everyone leaves. Even though you're tired, it's still better than waking up to the mess in the morning.

ZOMBIES AND OTHER HORRORS

According to voodoo, a "Zombie" is a supernatural power that brings the dead back to life. No wonder someone named a drink after that creature. Scares you to death, but gives you a second chance. Drinks called "Massacre" and "Terminator" are not nearly as "reviving." And who knows what to expect from a "Black Devil" or a "Banshee." But you don't believe in voodoo, do you?

Walking Zombie (Non-alcoholic)

2 oz.	fresh lime juice
2 oz.	fresh orange juice
2 oz.	pineapple juice
1 oz.	passion fruit syrup

Combine all ingredients in a blender with ice. Blend thoroughly. Pour into a collins or parfait glass. Garnish with a fruit slice, sprig of mint, and cherry. Serve with a straw

Zombie

2 oz.	light rum
1 oz.	dark rum
½ oz.	apricot brandy
½ oz.	151-proof rum
1 oz.	orange juice
1 oz.	pineapple juice
1 oz.	lime juice or juice of ½ lime
1 tsp.	sugar

Combine all ingredients except 151-proof rum in a blender with ice. Blend thoroughly. Pour into a collins or parfait glass. Float rum on top. Garnish with a fruit slice, sprig of mint, and cherry. Serve with a straw.

Black Devil

2 oz.	light rum
½ oz.	dry vermouth
	pitted black olive

Combine ingredients except olive in a shaker half filled with ice. Shake well. Strain into a cocktail glass. Garnish with the olive.

Dead Nazi Shooter

1 oz.	Jägermeister
1 oz.	peppermint schnapps

Pour ingredients into a mixing glass nearly filled with ice. Stir. Strain into a shot glass.

Banshee

2 oz.	crème de banane
1 oz.	white crème de cacao
1 oz.	light cream

Combine ingredients in a shaker half filled with ice. Shake well. Strain into a cocktail glass.

Nightmare

2 oz.	gin
1 oz.	Madeira
1/2 oz.	cherry brandy
1 Tbs.	orange juice

Combine ingredients in a shaker half filled with ice. Shake well. Strain into a cocktail glass.

Massacre

2 oz.	tequila
1/2 oz.	Campari
4 oz.	ginger ale

Combine all ingredients in a highball glass over ice. Stir well.

Brain Hemorrhage Shooter

3/4 oz.	coffee liqueur
3/4 oz.	vodka
splash	Irish cream liqueur
splash	grenadine

In a shaker half filled with ice, shake the coffee liqueur and vodka. Strain into a shot glass. "Swirl" the Irish cream and then the grenadine into the glass.

Buzzard's Breath Shooter

1/2 oz.	Amaretto
1/2 oz.	coffee liqueur
1/2 oz.	peppermint schnapps

Pour ingredients into a mixing glass nearly filled with ice. Stir. Strain into a shot glass.

Terminator Shooter

1/2 oz.	Jägermeister
1/2 oz.	Irish cream liqueur
1/2 oz.	peppermint schnapps
1/2 oz.	bourbon

Pour ingredients into a mixing glass nearly filled with ice. Stir. Strain into a shot glass.

A MENAGERIE IN A GLASS

In the 1940s, John Gilbert Martin of Heublein began producing vodka in America. He invented the "Moscow Mule," a drink of vodka and ginger beer, served in a copper mug, named for the liquor's Russian origins. "Moscow" makes sense, but why "Mule?" And why names like "Pink Squirrel" and "Hop Toad?" Why not? Drinks should be fun. Although a drink named "Rattlesnake" might not be for everyone.

Moscow Mule

1½ oz.	vodka
1 oz.	ginger beer
1 oz.	lime juice or juice of ½ lime

Pour ingredients into a highball glass nearly filled with ice. Stir well. Garnish with a wedge of lime.

Tiger's Milk

1 oz.	dark rum
1 oz.	brandy
4 oz..	milk
2 tsp.	fine sugar

Combine ingredients in a shaker half filled with ice. Shake well. Strain into an old-fashioned glass with ice.

Leap Frog

2 oz.	gin
1 oz.	lemon juice or juice of ½ lemon
	ginger ale

Pour gin and lemon juice into a highball glass nearly filled with ice. Add ginger ale. Stir.

Two Turtles

1½ oz.	Canadian whiskey
½ oz.	B & B
½ oz.	Cointreau

Pour ingredients into a mixing glass nearly filled with ice. Stir. Strain into a cocktail glass. Garnish with a cherry.

Hop Toad

¾ oz.	light rum
¾ oz.	apricot brandy
1 oz.	lime juice or juice of ½ lime

Pour ingredients into a mixing glass nearly filled with ice. Stir. Strain into a cocktail glass.

Pink Squirrel

1½ oz.	crème de noyaux
1 oz.	white crème de cacao
1 oz.	light cream

Combine ingredients in a shaker half filled with ice. Shake well. Strain into a cocktail glass.

Rattlesnake

2 oz.	blended whiskey
1 tsp.	Pernod
½ oz.	lemon juice
1 tsp.	fine sugar

Combine ingredients in a shaker half filled with ice. Shake well. Strain into a cocktail glass.

Iguana

1 oz.	tequila
1 oz.	coffee liqueur
1 oz.	vodka

Pour ingredients into a mixing glass nearly filled with ice. Stir. Strain into a cocktail glass.

Bullfrog

2 oz.	vodka
4 oz.	lemonade
1 tsp.	Cointreau

Pour ingredients into a highball or collins glass nearly filled with ice. Stir well. Garnish with a lemon wedge

Friendly Frog (Non-alcoholic)

1 oz.	lemon juice or juice of ½ lemon
1 tsp.	granulated sugar
3 oz.	chilled water
2 oz.	orange juice

Pour ingredients into a highball or collins glass nearly filled with ice. Stir well. Garnish with a lemon wedge

Part V
HOT STUFF AND COLD CONCOCTIONS

Tropical Drinks, Drinks Bearing Fruit, Frozen Drinks, Hot Drinks, Carousing with Coffee, Chocolate Ambrosia

BEAT THE HEAT: TROPICAL DRINKS

Picture palm trees swaying like dancers in the sultry night breeze, casting shadows on the sand in the moonlight. Think of languid afternoons on the beach, your eyes gazing on turquoise seas and the silence broken only by waves caressing the shore. And the tinkle of glasses. If you have a taste for fantasy, sip a tropical drink and heat up your imagination.

THE DAIQUIRI
. . . .

The Daiquiri is the doctor of drinks, having originated to fight an outbreak of malaria. The time was the turn of the century, the country was Cuba, the town was Daiquiri. Rum was the only substance available that physicians hoped would lower the malarial fever. So they mixed it up with lime and sugar to make the potion easier to take. *Very* easy to take, and just what the doctor ordered. The frozen daiquiri came later, just for the fun of it (see page 159).

Daiquiri

1½ oz.	light rum
1 oz.	lime juice or juice of ½ lime
1 tsp.	fine sugar

Combine rum, lime juice, and sugar in a shaker half filled with ice. Shake well. Strain into a cocktail glass.

Passionate Daiquiri

1½ oz.	light rum
1 oz.	lime juice or juice of ½ lime
½ oz.	passion fruit syrup

Combine rum, lime juice, and syrup in a shaker half filled with ice. Shake well. Strain into a cocktail glass.

Apple Daiquiri

1½ oz.	light rum
1 oz.	lime juice or juice of ½ lime
½ oz.	Calvados
1 tsp.	fine sugar

Combine ingredients in a shaker half filled with ice. Shake well. Strain into a cocktail glass. Garnish with an apple slice.

Mai Tai...Oh My!

A Mai Tai is a drink that begs for an umbrella, either one of those little paper ones jauntily set in the glass with a slice of pineapple, or a big shady one set on a sizzling beach. Choose the big one if you can.

2 oz.	light rum
1 oz.	Triple Sec
1 Tbs.	orgeat (almond) syrup
½ oz.	grenadine
1 oz.	lime juice or juice of ½ lime crushed ice

Combine all ingredients except crushed ice in a shaker half filled with ice. Shake well. Strain into an old-fashioned glass half filled with crushed ice. Garnish with a slice of fruit.

My Type
(Non-alcoholic)

3 oz.	orange juice
1 oz.	lime juice or juice of 1/2 lime
1 tsp.	fine sugar
1 Tbs.	orgeat (almond) syrup
1/2 oz.	grenadine
	crushed ice

Combine all ingredients except crushed ice in a shaker half filled with ice. Shake well. Strain into an old-fashioned glass half filled with crushed ice. Garnish with a slice of fruit.

The Salty Dog

When the weather's hot and the sun is blistering, take your dog for a swim in the ocean. Then you've got one salty dog. Mix yourself a cool, refreshing Salty Dog, and you've got another one. The better one.

1 1/2 oz.	vodka
4-5 oz.	grapefruit juice
	salt and lime to rim glass

Rim a highball glass with salt. Almost fill the glass with ice. Pour in the vodka and grapefruit juice and stir well.

The Salty Puppy
(Non-alcoholic)

4-5 oz.	grapefruit juice
	coarse salt
	fine sugar
	lime wedge

Rub rim of an old-fashioned glass with lime. Combine salt and sugar in a dish and dip the rim into the mixture. Pour grapefruit juice over ice.

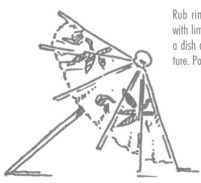

Tropical Wave

This drink is potent with possibilities. Almost any combination of liquors and juices will do. It's simply a matter of spirit (and spirits) and your own taste. Mix it up the way you like it and catch your own wave.

½ oz.	vodka
½ oz.	rum
½ oz.	gin
½ oz.	Triple Sec
½ oz.	grenadine
2 oz.	pineapple juice
1 oz.	cranberry juice

Combine any or all ingredients in a shaker half filled with ice. Shake well. Pour into a highball or collins glass over ice. Garnish with fruit.

Gentle Wave
(Non-alcoholic)

1½ oz.	pineapple juice
1½ oz.	cranberry juice
splash	orange juice
1 tsp.	grenadine
4 oz.	tonic water

Pour all ingredients except tonic into a collins glass over ice. Stir well. Add tonic. Stir. Garnish with fruit.

Planter's Punch

The lively sound of steel drums echoing up and down the Caribbean is the siren song of Planter's Punch, the welcoming melody of the islands. Like the drum's rhythmic beat, the drink is hypnotic, meant to be sipped with the slow pace of the tropics.

2 oz.	light rum
1 oz.	dark rum
1 oz.	lime juice or juice of ½ lime
1 oz.	lemon juice or juice of ½ lemon
2 oz.	orange juice
1 oz.	pineapple juice
1 dash	Triple Sec
1 dash	grenadine fruit to garnish

Combine all ingredients except the Triple Sec and grenadine in a shaker half filled with ice. Shake well. Pour into a highball glass nearly filled with ice. Top with Triple Sec and grenadine. Garnish with slices of orange and pineapple, wedges of lemon and lime, and a cherry.

Planter's Punch (Non-alcoholic)

1 tsp.	Rose's lime juice
1 tsp.	lemon juice
3 oz.	orange juice
2 oz.	pineapple juice
1 oz.	grapefruit juice
1 tsp.	powdered sugar
1 dash	grenadine
	fruit to garnish

Combine all ingredients except grenadine in a shaker half filled with ice. Shake well. Pour into a highball glass nearly filled with ice. Top with grenadine. Garnish with slices of orange and pineapple, wedges of lemon and lime, and a cherry.

Tahiti Club

1 oz.	light rum
1 oz.	dark rum
2 oz.	pineapple juice
1 tsp.	lemon juice or juice of ½ lemon
1 tsp.	lime juice or juice of ½ lime
1 tsp.	Maraschino

Combine all ingredients in a shaker half filled with ice. Shake well. Strain into an old-fashioned glass nearly filled with ice. Garnish with fruit.

Caribbean Breeze

2 oz.	dark rum
½ oz.	Cointreau
½ oz.	crème de banane
1 tsp.	Rose's lime juice
1 tsp.	grenadine
4 oz.	pineapple juice

Combine all ingredients in a shaker half filled with ice. Shake well. Strain into a collins or highball glass nearly filled with ice. Garnish with fruit.

South Pacific (Non-alcoholic)

2 oz.	orange juice concentrate
½ oz.	lemonade concentrate
1½ oz.	cranberry juice, chilled
2 tsp.	fine sugar
2 ½ oz.	water
1½ oz.	Hawaiian Punch, chilled
1 quarter	banana, sliced
¼ cup	strawberries

Blend banana, strawberries, juice concentrates, sugar, and water in blender until smooth. Pour into a highball or collins glass. Add cranberry juice and Hawaiian Punch. Stir well. Garnish with fruit.

Reggae

2 oz.	vodka
1/2 oz.	crème de banane
1 oz.	orange juice
1 oz.	pineapple juice
1 oz.	grapefruit juice
1 tsp.	grenadine
dash	bitters

Combine all ingredients in a shaker half filled with ice. Shake well. Strain into a collins or highball glass nearly filled with ice. Garnish with fruit.

Hairless Reggae (Non-alcoholic)

1/2 oz.	banana, sliced
1 oz.	orange juice
1 oz.	pineapple juice
1 oz.	grapefruit juice
1 tsp.	grenadine

Mash banana. Combine with juices and grenadine in a shaker half filled with ice. Shake well. Strain into a collins or highball glass nearly filled with ice. Garnish with fruit.

Yellow Bird

1 1/2 oz.	light rum
1/2 oz.	Galliano
1/2 oz.	Triple Sec
1/2 oz.	lime juice

Combine all ingredients in a shaker half filled with ice. Shake well. Strain into a cocktail glass.

Tropical Gold

1 oz.	rum
1/2 oz.	crème de banane
5 oz.	orange juice

Combine ingredients in a shaker half filled with ice. Shake well. Strain into a highball glass over ice. Garnish with an orange slice.

Honolulu Hammer Shooter

Here's a shooter to hammer home that tropical feeling.

1 1/2 oz.	vodka
1/2 oz.	Amaretto
splash	pineapple juice

Stir in a mixing glass and pour into a shot glass.

DRINKS BEARING FRUIT

When Eve bit into the apple, there was trouble. Today, fruit is the sinless alternative. Naturally sweet, low in calories, and high in fiber, fruit makes a perfect drink. Well, almost. A combination of fruit and liquor is sublime. A touch of apple, banana, peach, or cranberry and a drink becomes flavorful, even ambrosial. Eve would not be able to resist. Again.

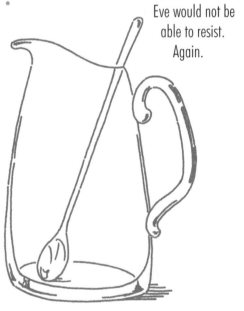

Apple Blossom

2 oz.	brandy
2 oz.	apple juice
1 tsp.	lemon juice or juice of ½ lemon

Pour ingredients into a mixing glass nearly filled with ice. Stir. Strain into an old-fashioned glass over ice. Garnish with fruit.

Lemony Apple (Non-alcoholic)

3 oz.	apple juice
1 oz.	lemon juice or juice of ½ lemon
1 oz.	grenadine
8 oz.	ginger ale

Pour apple and lemon juice in a collins or highball glass. Stir. Add ginger ale. Drizzle in grenadine.

Woo Woo Shooter

1 oz.	cranberry juice
½ oz.	Amaretto
½ oz.	peach-flavored brandy

Pour ingredients into a shaker nearly filled with ice. Shake. Strain into a shot glass.

Apricot Fizz

2 oz.	apricot-flavored brandy
1 tsp.	lemon juice or juice of ½ lemon
1 tsp.	lime juice or juice of ½ lime
1 tsp.	fine sugar club soda

Combine brandy, juices, and sugar in a shaker half filled with ice. Shake well. Strain into an old-fashioned glass with only a few ice cubes. Add club soda. Stir gently.

Apricot Sparkler (Non-alcoholic)

| 2 oz. | apricot nectar |
| 1 oz. | lemon juice or juice of ½ lemon club soda |

Combine juices in a shaker half filled with ice. Shake well. Strain into an old-fashioned glass with only a few ice cubes. Add club soda and stir gently. Add a lemon twist.

Banana Rum Frappe

1½ oz.	light rum
½ oz.	banana liqueur
½ oz.	orange juice

Combine ingredients in a blender with ice. Blend thoroughly. Pour into a collins or parfait glass.

Banana Orange Smoothy (Non-alcoholic)

1	banana
¾ cup	orange juice
1 Tbs.	lemon juice
	banana slice

Combine ingredients in a blender with ice. Blend thoroughly. Pour into a collins or parfait glass. Garnish with banana.

Peaches and Cream

| 2 oz. | peach liqueur |
| 2 oz. | light cream |

Combine ingredients in a shaker half filled with ice. Shake well. Strain into an old-fashioned glass over ice.

Banana Cow

1½ oz.	light rum
1 oz.	crème de banane
1 oz.	cream
	banana slice

Combine ingredients in a shaker half filled with ice. Shake well. Strain into a cocktail glass. Garnish with banana.

Banana Shake (Non-alcoholic)

½ cup	low fat milk
½ cup	low fat plain yogurt
one half	banana
¼ tsp.	vanilla

Combine ingredients in a blender without ice. Blend thoroughly. Pour into a collins or parfait glass.

Peach Bunny

1 oz.	peach-flavored brandy
¾ oz.	white crème de cacao
¾ oz.	light cream

Combine ingredients in a shaker half filled with ice. Shake well. Strain into a cordial glass.

Creamy Peach
(Non-alcoholic)

1	peach or 2 oz. frozen peaches
1 tsp.	sugar
1 oz.	light cream lemonade, chilled

Peel and cut up peach if fresh. Put into a blender and blend well. Add sugar to taste. Pour into a collins glass and add cream. Stir well. Add lemonade. Stir. Garnish with peach.

Cranberry Gin Sour

2 oz.	gin
½ oz.	Triple Sec
1 oz.	lime juice or juice of ½ lime
1 oz.	lemon juice or juice of ½ lemon
2 oz.	light cream
1 tsp.	sugar

Combine ingredients in a blender with ice. Blend thoroughly. Pour into a large wine glass.

Cranberry Cream
Cocktail
(Non-alcoholic)

3 oz.	cranberry juice
2 oz.	apple juice
1 oz.	lime juice or juice of ½ lime
1 oz.	cream
dash	grenadine

Combine ingredients in a blender with ice. Blend thoroughly. Pour into a large wine glass.

Melon Ball

1 oz.	vodka
2 oz.	melon liqueur
4 oz.	pineapple juice

Pour ingredients into a mixing glass nearly filled with ice. Stir. Strain into a highball or collins glass over ice. Garnish with fruit.

Melon Marvel
(Non-alcoholic)

1 wedge	cantaloupe, cubed (6 oz.)
½ cup	orange juice
½ oz.	lime juice
splash	club soda

Combine ingredients in a blender without ice. Blend thoroughly. Pour into a collins or parfait glass. Add a splash of club soda. Stir well.

Raspberry Romance

1 oz.	black raspberry liqueur
1 oz.	coffee liqueur
1½ oz.	Irish cream liqueur
	club soda

Pour liqueurs over ice into a collins or parfait glass. Stir. Add club soda to fill. Stir gently.

Raspberry Cloud
(Non-alcoholic)

¼ cup	raspberries, fresh or frozen
1 oz.	milk
1 Tbs.	honey

Put berries in a blender and blend well. Add milk, honey and 2 ice cubes. Blend completely. Pour into a large wine glass.

Orange Buck

1½ oz.	gin
2 oz.	orange juice
1 oz.	lime juice or juice of ½ lime
	ginger ale

Combine all ingredients except ginger ale in a shaker half filled with ice. Shake well. Strain into a collins or highball glass over ice. Garnish with lime.

Orange Fizz
(Non-alcoholic)

2 oz.	orange juice
2 oz.	sparkling white grape juice
	lime wedge

Pour into a large wine glass over ice. Squeeze lime and add to drink.

Passion Cup

2 oz.	vodka
2 oz.	orange juice
1 oz.	passion fruit juice
½ oz.	coconut cream
	maraschino cherry

Combine ingredients in a shaker half filled with ice. Shake well. Strain into a large wine glass. Top with a cherry

Night of Passion
(Non-alcoholic)

2 oz.	passion fruit juice
1 oz.	orange juice
1 oz.	pineapple juice
2 Tbs.	cream
1	egg yolk
dash	club soda
	crushed ice

Combine ingredients in a shaker half filled with ice. Shake well. Strain into a wine glass over crushed ice. Serve with a straw.

Very Cherry

³/₄ oz.	white crème de cacao
³/₄ oz.	Amaretto
³/₄ oz.	light cream
6	maraschino cherries
¹/₂ oz.	maraschino cherry juice

Combine ingredients in a blender with ice. Blend thoroughly. Pour into a collins or parfait glass. Garnish with a cherry. Serve with a straw.

Creamy Cherry
(Non-alcoholic)

4 oz.	cherry soda
2 scoops	vanilla ice cream

Combine ingredients in a blender without ice. Blend thoroughly. Pour into a collins or parfait glass. Garnish with a cherry. Serve with a straw.

Strawberry Sunrise

2 oz.	strawberry liqueur
1 oz.	grenadine
3 oz.	orange juice

Pour into a highball glass over ice. Stir well. Garnish with fruit.

Strawberry Dawn
(Non-alcoholic)

¹/₄ cup	strawberries, fresh or frozen
1 oz.	orange juice
1 tsp.	sugar or to taste
	orange-flavored sparkling water
	orange twist

Combine berries, juice, and sugar in a blender without ice. Blend well. Pour into a large wine glass. Add sparkling water to fill and an orange twist.

Pineapple Fizz

2 oz.	rum
2 oz.	pineapple juice
1 tsp.	fine sugar
	club soda

Combine ingredients except club soda in a shaker half filled with ice. Shake well. Strain into a collins or highball glass. Add soda. Stir gently.

Pink Pineapple
(Non-alcoholic)

4 oz.	pineapple juice
3 oz.	cherry soda

Pour into a highball or collins glass. Mix slightly. Garnish with fruit.

FROZEN DRINKS: ICE IS NICE BUT BLENDED IS BETTER

Slurp it with a straw, eat it with a spoon, a frozen or blended drink is the candy of bartending. Like dessert, no one can resist one of these freezing concoctions. To mix a blended drink all you need is a willingness to forego the purity of a crisp, stringently measured cocktail for the froth of spirits and fruit chaotically churned together. It's the difference between a brisk shower and a bubble bath.

A blender is essential and instructions are simple: Begin with the motor off. Add ingredients in this order: liquor, mixers, fruit, and ice until the pitcher is three-quarters full. The more ice, the thicker the drink will be. Close and blend. Start at low speed and switch to high. Indulge.

COLADAS: COCONUT AND BEYOND
. . . .

Delicious piña coladas and sun-drenched settings seem to go together. There's no question that being with the coconut on its native ground is the most enjoyable way to indulge in a colada. But you can also stop at the supermarket, pick up a can of coconut cream, and bring a little sunshine home. Mix it up with fruit and you've got a colada for whatever you crave.

Piña Colada

2 oz.	light rum
2 oz.	coconut cream
4 oz.	pineapple juice

Combine all ingredients in a blender in this order: rum, coconut cream, juice, and ice. Blend thoroughly. Pour into a collins or parfait glass. Serve with a pineapple slice, a cherry, and a straw.

Coy Colada
(Non-alcoholic)

2 oz.	coconut cream
6 oz.	pineapple juice
1 tsp.	lime juice

Combine ingredients in a blender with ice. Blend thoroughly. Pour into a collins or parfait glass. Serve with a pineapple slice, a cherry, and a straw.

Banana Colada

2 oz.	rum
2 oz.	coconut cream
1	banana, sliced
4 oz.	pineapple juice

Combine all ingredients in a blender in this order: rum, coconut cream, banana, pineapple juice, and ice. Blend thoroughly. Pour into a collins or parfait glass. Serve with a pineapple slice, a cherry, and a straw.

Anna Banana Colada
(Non-alcoholic)

1½ oz.	coconut cream
1	banana, sliced
5 oz.	pineapple juice

Combine ingredients in a blender with ice. Blend thoroughly. Pour into a collins or parfait glass. Serve with a pineapple slice, a cherry, and a straw.

Midori Colada

1 oz.	Midori
1 oz.	light rum
2 oz.	coconut cream
4 oz.	pineapple juice

Combine all ingredients in a blender in this order: Midori, rum, coconut cream, pineapple juice, and ice. Blend thoroughly. Pour into a collins or parfait glass. Serve with a pineapple or melon slice, a cherry, and a straw.

Nutty Colada

3 oz.	Amaretto
2 oz.	coconut cream
3 oz.	pineapple juice

Combine ingredients in a blender with ice. Blend thoroughly. Pour into a collins or parfait glass. Serve with a straw.

Strawberry Colada

2 oz.	rum
1 oz.	coconut cream
½ cup	strawberries, fresh or frozen
4 oz.	pineapple juice

Combine all ingredients in a blender in this order: rum, coconut cream, strawberries, pineapple juice, and ice. Blend thoroughly. Pour into a collins or parfait glass. Serve with a pineapple slice or strawberry and a straw.

Virgin Strawberry Colada (Non-alcoholic)

1½ oz.	coconut cream
½ cup	strawberries, fresh or frozen
5 oz.	pineapple juice

Combine ingredients in a blender with ice. Blend thoroughly. Pour into a collins or parfait glass. Serve with a pineapple slice or a strawberry and a straw.

DAIQUIRIS
• • • • • • • • • • • • • • • • • •

The elegant daiquiri appears on page 145, but the frozen version is something else, a light froth, a frivolity. Whipped up with ice, the daiquiri becomes a confection. Add a fruit of your choice and you have an indulgence.

Frozen Daiquiri

2 oz.	rum
1/2 oz.	Triple Sec
1 oz.	lime juice or juice of 1/2 lime
1 tsp.	fine sugar

Combine ingredients in a blender with ice. Blend thoroughly. Pour into a collins or parfait glass. Garnish with a slice of lime. Serve with a straw.

Frozen Peach Daiquiri

2 oz.	rum
1/2 oz.	peach-flavored brandy
1 oz.	lime juice or juice of 1/2 lime
1	canned peach half
1 tsp.	fine sugar

Combine ingredients in a blender with ice. Blend thoroughly. Pour into a collins or parfait glass. Serve with a straw.

Frozen Pineapple Daiquiri

2 oz.	rum
1/2 oz.	Triple Sec
1 oz.	lime juice or juice of 1/2 lime
1 tsp.	fine sugar
1/2 cup	pineapple chunks

Combine all ingredients in a blender in this order: rum, Triple Sec, lime juice, sugar, pineapple, and ice. Blend thoroughly. Pour into a collins or parfait glass. Serve with a straw.

Frozen Banana Daiquiri

2 oz.	rum
1/2 oz.	Triple Sec
1 oz.	lime juice or juice of 1/2 lime
1 tsp.	fine sugar
1	banana, sliced

Combine all ingredients in a blender in this order: rum, Triple Sec, lime juice, sugar, banana, and ice. Blend thoroughly. Pour into a collins or parfait glass. Serve with a straw.

Frozen Strawberry Daiquiri

2 oz.	rum
½ oz.	Triple Sec
1 oz.	lime juice or juice of ½ lime
1 tsp.	fine sugar
½ cup	strawberries, fresh or frozen

Combine all ingredients in a blender in this order: rum, Triple Sec, lime juice, sugar, strawberries, and ice. Blend thoroughly. Pour into a collins or parfait glass. Serve with a straw.

Virgin Strawberry Daiquiri (Non-alcoholic)

¼ cup	strawberries
1 oz.	orange juice
1 oz.	lime juice or juice of ½ lime
2 tsp.	sugar
dash	grenadine

Combine all ingredients in a blender with ice. Blend well. Pour into a stemmed glass. Garnish with fruit.

FROZEN MARGARITA
• • • • • • • • • • • • • • • • • • •

The Margarita in its frozen form is not just an ambrosial delight. It's made to stand up to the whirling blender of ice. Assertive. Tangy. Lively. And salty. Don't forget the salt.

2 oz.	tequila
1 oz.	Triple Sec
2 oz.	lemon or lime juice
1-2 tsp.	fine sugar
	salt and lime wedge to rim glass

Combine all ingredients in a blender in this order: tequila, Triple Sec, lime juice, sugar, and ice. Blend thoroughly. Pour into a large wine glass.

Frozen Strawberry Margarita

2 oz.	tequila
1 oz.	Triple Sec
3 oz.	lemon or lime juice
½ cup	strawberries, fresh or frozen
1-2 tsp.	fine sugar
	salt and lime wedge to rim glass

Combine all ingredients in a blender in this order: tequila, Triple Sec, lime juice, strawberries, sugar, and ice. Blend thoroughly. Pour into a large wine glass.

Lava Flow (Non-alcoholic)

3 oz.	milk
½ oz.	coconut cream
3 oz.	pineapple juice
½	banana
½ cup	strawberries, fresh or frozen

Combine all ingredients in a blender in this order: milk, coconut cream, pineapple juice, banana, strawberries, and ice. Blend thoroughly. Pour into a collins or parfait glass. Serve with a straw.

Gauguin

2 oz.	light rum
1 oz.	passion fruit syrup
1 tsp.	lime juice or juice of ½ lime
1 tsp.	grenadine
½ tsp.	fine sugar

Combine ingredients in a blender and blend thoroughly. Pour into a collins or parfait glass. Garnish with fruit. Serve with a straw.

Cool Operator

1 oz.	Midori
½ oz.	rum
½ oz.	vodka
1 oz.	lime juice or juice of ½ lime
2 oz.	grapefruit juice
4 oz.	orange juice

Combine ingredients in a blender and blend thoroughly. Pour into a collins or parfait glass. Garnish with fruit. Serve with a straw.

Slow Operator (Non-alcoholic)

1 oz.	lime juice or juice of ½ lime
3 oz.	grapefruit juice
4 oz.	orange juice
1 tsp.	fine sugar

Combine ingredients in a blender with ice and blend thoroughly. Pour into a collins or parfait glass. Garnish with fruit. Serve with a straw.

HOT DRINKS: A CUP OF WARMTH

Winter comes upon us from the weather and sometimes from the soul. And there's no better antidote than a steaming drink with a mug to warm your hands. Guaranteed to ease what ails you, a hot drink is a pick-me-up or an ease-me-down. These drinks include wine and whiskey, spices and chocolate—something that will work for everyone.

Steaming Bull

2 oz.	tequila
2 oz.	beef bouillon
4 oz.	tomato juice
splash	lime juice
dash	Worcestershire sauce

Heat all ingredients except tequila in a saucepan. Do not boil. Pour into mug and add tequila.

Hot Sultry Zoë

1 oz.	tequila
½ oz.	Galliano
5 oz.	hot chocolate
2 oz.	cream

Pour tequila, Galliano, and hot chocolate into an Irish Coffee glass or mug. Stir gently. Add cream by pouring it over the back of a spoon so that it floats on top.

Hot Wine Lemonade

1½ oz.	red wine
1 oz.	lemon juice or juice of ½ lemon
1 Tbs.	fine sugar
4 oz.	boiling water

In an Irish Coffee glass or mug, dissolve sugar in a splash of water. Add the wine and lemon juice. Stir. Fill with water. Stir well. Garnish with a lemon twist.

Hot Toddy

2 oz.	bourbon
4 oz.	boiling water
1 Tbs.	fine sugar
splash	lemon juice
dash	ground cloves
dash	cinnamon

In a coffee mug, dissolve the sugar and spices in 1 oz. of the boiling water. Stir. Add the lemon juice, bourbon, and the rest of the water. Stir well.

Hot Not Toddy (Non-alcoholic)

6 oz.	hot tea
1 Tbs.	honey
splash	lemon juice
dash	ground cloves
dash	cinnamon
dash	nutmeg (optional)

In a coffee mug, dissolve the honey and spices in 1 oz. of tea. Stir. Add the lemon juice and the rest of the tea. Stir well.

Chimney Fire

1½ oz.	Amaretto
4 oz.	hot cider
	cinnamon

Pour ingredients into an Irish Coffee glass or mug. Stir. Sprinkle with cinnamon.

Mulled Wine

6 oz.	red wine
splash	brandy
1 Tbs.	fine sugar
splash	lemon juice
2 whole	cloves
1 dash	cinnamon

Combine ingredients in a saucepan and heat to simmer. Do not boil. Stir well. Pour into a coffee mug.

Mulled Cranberry Juice (Non-alcoholic)

6 oz.	cranberry juice
splash	lemon juice
1 tsp.	honey or more to taste
2 whole	cloves
dash	nutmeg

Combine ingredients in a saucepan and heat to simmer. Do not boil. Stir well. Pour into a coffee mug.

Gluhwein

6 oz.	red wine
1 tsp.	honey or to taste
1	cinnamon stick
1	lemon slice
1	orange slice
3	cloves
dash	nutmeg

Combine ingredients in a saucepan and heat to simmer. Do not boil. Pour into a mug.

Hot Buttered Rum

2 oz.	rum
1½ tsp.	brown sugar
1 tsp.	cinnamon
1 Tbs.	butter
4 oz.	milk
dash	salt
	nutmeg

Heat milk in a saucepan, being careful not to boil. Combine sugar, cinnamon, and salt in a mug. Add rum and butter. Pour in hot milk. Sprinkle with nutmeg.

● ●

Espresso Explained

● ●

The perfect cup of coffee is no longer just a simple brew. With latte and cappuccino, coffee can be as rich in flavor and complex in texture as dessert. These delicious permutations begin with espresso, the soul of coffee. Home espresso machines now make possible what Italians invented in 1903. They came up with the method and machines for forcing hot water at high pressure through very finely ground coffee. The result is an intense potion with a golden froth and a deeply satisfying aroma. It is drunk in a small cup, almost like a shot, a fleeting inhalation of hot liquid. Indeed, a "shot" of espresso is the foundation for a variety of specialty drinks. Most require steamed or foamed milk, achieved in a simple step with a machine attachment.

Espresso Macchiato: One shot of espresso with a dollop of foamed milk added.
Caffe Mocha: Enough chocolate syrup to cover the bottom of the cup. Then pour one shot of espresso, and add steamed milk almost to the rim of the cup. A dollop of whipped cream finishes the top.
Caffe Latte: One shot of espresso. Steamed milk almost to the rim of the cup. One quarter inch of foamed milk on top.
Cappuccino: One shot of espresso. Steamed milk to fill one half of the cup. Foamed milk up to and over the top.
Caffe Americano: One shot of espresso. Add boiling water to nearly fill the cup.

● ●

CAROUSING WITH COFFEE

Jamaican, Javan, Colombian, Kenyan. Gourmet and fresh ground, coffee is hot. No longer just for sipping, coffee is an object of desire for tasting, discussing, comparing, and coveting. So invite friends over for coffee and give them something to really talk about—"Monk's Coffee" with Frangelico, "Anatole Coffee" with cognac, "Coffee Royale" with bourbon, and a coffee called "Five before Flying" for an entirely unprecedented coffee experience.

Five before Flying

½ oz.	bourbon
½ oz.	Southern Comfort
½ oz.	crème de banane
½ oz.	white crème de cacao
4 oz.	hot coffee
2 oz.	heavy cream

Pour all ingredients except the cream into a mug or Irish Coffee glass. Stir. Add cream by pouring over the back of a spoon so that it floats on top.

Coffee Nut Sundae

1 oz.	Amaretto
½ oz.	Frangelico
	hot black coffee
	whipped cream

Pour ingredients except whipped cream into an Irish Coffee glass or mug. Stir. Top with whipped cream.

Café au Lait (Non-alcoholic)

hot coffee
hot milk
sugar to taste

Combine equal parts of coffee and milk. Add sugar. Stir.

Coffee Cacao Cream

½ cup	crème de cacao
½ cup	coffee
1 scoop	coffee ice cream

Combine ingredients in a blender without ice. Pour into a highball or parfait glass. Serve with a straw.

Coffee Almond Float (Non-alcoholic)

¼ cup	coffee
1 tsp.	brown sugar
splash	orgeat (almond) syrup
	milk
1 scoop	coffee or chocolate ice cream

Dissolve brown sugar in coffee in a highball or parfait glass. Add orgeat. Add ice and milk. Stir well. Top with a scoop of ice cream.

Coffee Royale

2 oz.	brandy
4 oz.	hot coffee
1 tsp.	granulated sugar
2 oz.	heavy cream

Dissolve sugar in coffee in a mug or Irish Coffee glass. Add brandy. Stir. Add cream by pouring over the back of a spoon so that it floats on top.

Monk's Coffee

1½ oz.	Frangelico
½ oz.	dark crème de cacao
4 oz.	hot coffee
2 oz.	heavy cream

Pour all ingredients except the cream into a mug or Irish Coffee glass. Stir. Add cream by pouring over the back of a spoon so that it floats on top.

Anatole Coffee

½ oz.	cognac
½ oz.	coffee liqueur
½ oz.	Frangelico
	iced coffee
	whipped cream

Combine ingredients except whipped cream in a blender with ice. Blend thoroughly. Pour into a large wine glass. Top with whipped cream.

Coffee Grasshopper

1 oz.	coffee liqueur
1 oz.	white crème de menthe
1 oz.	light cream

Combine ingredients in a shaker half filled with ice. Shake well. Strain into an old-fashioned glass over ice.

CHOCOLATE: AMBROSIA OF THE GODS

Many people believe that chocolate is divine, but the ancient Aztecs knew for sure. Their great, benevolent god Quetzalcoatl brought them the seeds of the cocoa tree...and the rest is history. Cortés the Conquistador brought chocolate to Europe in its first incarnation, a frothy, intoxicating drink. The nobles kept it to themselves, believing it to be too decadent for the masses. They may have been right. Drinking it is the only way to find out.

Comfort Mocha

1½ oz.	Southern Comfort
1 tsp.	instant cocoa
1 tsp.	instant coffee
	whipped cream

Pour Southern Comfort into an Irish Coffee glass. Add the dry ingredients. Fill with boiling water. Top with whipped cream.

Chocolate Vice

1½ oz.	light rum
½ oz.	bourbon
½ oz.	dark crème de cacao
4 oz.	hot chocolate
	whipped cream

Pour all the ingredients except cream into an Irish Coffee glass. Top with whipped cream.

Death by Chocolate

1 oz.	vodka
½ oz.	dark crème de cacao
½ oz.	Irish cream liqueur
1 scoop	vanilla ice cream

Combine ingredients in a blender with ice. Blend thoroughly. Pour into a collins or parfait glass. Garnish with chocolate shavings.

Chocolate Covered Strawberry

1 oz.	strawberry liqueur
1 oz.	white crème de cacao
½ oz.	cream

Pour ingredients into a mixing glass nearly filled with ice. Stir. Strain into a red wine glass over ice.

Chocolate Dipped Strawberry (Non-alcoholic)

2 oz.	strawberry soda
1 Tbs.	chocolate syrup
1 oz.	light cream

Pour chocolate and cream into a mixing glass nearly filled with ice. Stir. Strain into a red wine glass over ice. Add soda. Stir gently.

Chocolate Mint Rum

1 oz.	light rum
½ oz.	dark crème de cacao
½ oz.	white crème de menthe
½ oz.	light cream

Combine ingredients in a shaker half filled with ice. Shake well. Strain into a cocktail glass. Often served in an old-fashioned glass over ice.

Chocolate Almond Cream

Here's a drink that serves more than one. Perhaps. For true chocolate addicts, one is never enough.

½ cup	Amaretto
¼ cup	dark crème de cacao
¼ cup	white crème de cacao
1 quart	vanilla ice cream

Combine ingredients in a blender with ice. Blend thoroughly. Pour into a collins or parfait glass. Garnish with shaved chocolate.

Chocolate-Banana Supreme

1½ oz.	Irish cream liqueur
¼ oz.	vanilla extract
½ oz.	light cream
½ scoop	chocolate ice cream
one half	banana

Combine ingredients in a blender with a small amount of crushed ice. Blend until smooth. Pour into a collins or parfait glass. Garnish with a cherry and banana.

Tootsie Roll

1½ oz.	coffee liqueur
1½ oz.	dark crème de cacao
3 oz.	milk

Combine ingredients in a shaker half filled with ice. Shake well. Strain into a highball glass over ice.

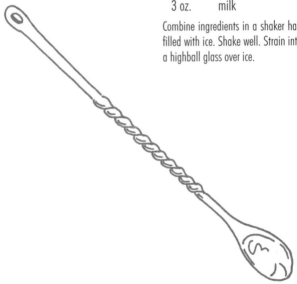

PART VI

HOLIDAYS AND SPECIAL DAYS—THEME DRINKS FOR EVERY OCCASION

Punch, Holidays: Valentine's Day, Saint Pat's, 4th of July, Halloween, Thanksgiving, Christmas, New Year's Eve, Parties: Beach Blast, Mexican Mayhem, Derby Drinks, Southern Soiree, Hawaiian Luau

PUNCH: THE CROWD PLEASER

Summer or winter, fruity or spicy, cold or hot, alcoholic or non-alcoholic, sparkling or not, punch is always a crowd pleaser. Gather people around a punch bowl and they become sociable, downright convivial. For cold punches, a ring of ice made in a jello mold works better than ice cubes. Take these recipes as gospel, or improvise. Please yourself. The crowd will follow.

Fish House Punch

1 bottle	peach brandy
1 bottle	light rum
2 bottles	dry white wine
1 quart	club soda or sparkling water
1½ cups	lemon juice
½ cup	fine sugar

Dissolve sugar in lemon juice and brandy. Add rum and wine. Stir. Refrigerate. Pour into a punch bowl over ice. Add club soda just before serving. Approximately 25 servings.

Claret Cup

2 bottles	dry red wine
½ cup	blackberry brandy
½ cup	Triple Sec
½ cup	lemon juice
1 cup	orange juice
2 Tbs.	grenadine sliced fruit

Combine ingredients and pour into a punch bowl over ice. Garnish with fruit. Approximately 15 servings.

Cape Cod Punch

3 cups	vodka
2 quarts	cranberry juice
1 quart	orange juice
½ cup	lemon juice
½ cup	fine sugar
1 quart	mineral water

Dissolve sugar in juices in a large bowl. Add vodka. Stir well. Pour over ice into a punch bowl. Add water before serving. Approximately 30 servings.

Bishop's Punch

2 bottles	sweet red wine
¼ cup	cognac
4	oranges studded with cloves
¼ tsp.	cinnamon
¼ tsp.	nutmeg

Bake oranges on a cookie sheet in a 400 degree oven for 30 minutes or until soft. Heat liquors and spices, but do not boil. Place the oranges in a punch bowl. Add wine and cognac. Approximately 12 servings.

Rhine Wine Punch

1 bottle	Rhine wine
1/2 cup	brandy
1/2 cup	Cointreau
1 cup	orange juice
1 bottle	sparkling white wine, chilled

Combine all ingredients except sparkling wine. Pour into a punch bowl over ice. Stir well. Add sparkling wine just before serving. Approximately 15 servings.

Ruby Red Wine Punch

1 bottle	red wine
1 cup	lemon juice
3/4 cup	fine sugar
1 cup	raspberry syrup
1 quart	club soda

Combine all ingredients except club soda. Stir to make sure sugar is dissolved. Pour into a punch bowl over ice. Stir well. Add soda just before serving. Approximately 20 servings.

Raspberry Punch (Non-alcoholic)

2 quarts	cran-raspberry drink
1 quart	raspberry soda, chilled
10 oz.	frozen raspberries, thawed, with juice
1 quart	raspberry sherbet

Combine all ingredients except soda. Pour into a punch bowl over ice. Stir well. Add soda just before serving. Approximately 20 servings.

Whiskey Punch

1 liter	bourbon
1/2 cup	Curaçao
2 cups	orange juice
1/2 cup	lemon juice
2 quarts	ginger ale
	maraschino cherries

Combine all ingredients except ginger ale. Pour into a punch bowl over ice. Stir well. Add ginger ale just before serving. Approximately 20 servings.

Flavor of Fruit Punch

1 liter	vodka
1 bottle	white wine
2 (12 oz.)	cans of fruit juice concentrate, thawed
2 quarts	club soda

Combine all ingredients except club soda. Pour into a punch bowl over ice. Stir well. Add soda just before serving. Approximately 35 servings.

Personal Punch (Non-alcoholic)

10 oz.	frozen strawberries
2 cups	orange juice
2 cups	pineapple juice
1 (12 oz.)	can of frozen juice concentrate (any flavor)
3 cups	water
2 bottles	sparkling water

Thaw strawberries and purée them in a blender. Combine all ingredients except sparkling water in a punch bowl over ice. Add sparkling water just before serving. Garnish with fruit. Approximately 20 servings.

SPIRITED HOLIDAYS

Holidays only come once a year—every year. We look forward to their rituals and traditions and recognize their importance in our lives. But they should be fun. To keep them fresh and lively, entertaining and interesting, requires some inventiveness...and spirits. So here are a few suggestions to make your holidays much more spirited.

VALENTINE'S DAY
• • • • • • • • • • • • • • • • •

The perfect Valentine's Day party may be just for two. Even three can be a crowd. But if more is merrier, be ready with drinks for all your guests' romantic or unromantic circumstances. For the determinedly single, there's the "Confirmed Bachelor." For the amorous, try a "Cherry Kiss." Give serious couples a nudge with a "Wedding Belle." And for the jilted, the lonely, the searching, and the jealous, the drink of the day is definitely "Stupid Cupid."

Stupid Cupid

1½ oz.	vodka
½ oz.	sloe gin
1 oz.	lemon juice or juice of ½ lemon

Pour ingredients into a mixing glass nearly filled with ice. Stir. Strain into a cocktail glass. Garnish with a cherry.

Pink Valentine Punch

1 bottle	champagne, chilled
1 bottle	rosé wine
10 oz.	frozen strawberries, thawed
¼ cup	fine sugar

Place sugar and strawberries (with their juice) in punch bowl. Stir to dissolve sugar. Add wine and champagne. Approximately 15 servings.

Confirmed Bachelor

1½ oz.	gin
1 tsp.	Rose's lime juice
1 tsp.	grenadine
1	egg white

Combine ingredients in a shaker half filled with ice. Shake well. Strain into a cocktail glass.

Seething Jealousy

1 oz.	sweet vermouth
1 oz.	scotch
½ oz.	cherry brandy
½ oz.	orange juice

Combine ingredients in a shaker half filled with ice. Shake well. Strain into a cocktail glass.

Pink Lady

2 oz.	gin
1 tsp.	cherry brandy
1 tsp.	grenadine
1 tsp.	light cream
1	egg white

Combine ingredients in a shaker half filled with ice. Shake well. Strain into a cocktail glass.

Cherry Kiss

| 1 oz. | Irish cream liqueur |
| 1 oz. | Chambord |

Use a pousse-café or cordial glass. Pour Irish cream liqueur first. Then add Chambord by pouring it over the back of a spoon so that it floats on top.

Wedding Belle

1½ oz.	gin
1 oz.	Dubonnet rouge
½ oz.	Kirschwasser
½ oz.	orange juice

Combine ingredients in a shaker half filled with ice. Shake well. Strain into a cocktail glass.

Frozen Pink Valentine (Non-alcoholic)

4 oz.	cranberry juice
¼ cup	raspberries, fresh or frozen
1 scoop	vanilla ice cream

Put all ingredients in a blender and blend. Pour into a collins or parfait glass. Serve with a straw.

Honeymoon

1 oz.	apple brandy
1 oz.	Benedictine
1 tsp.	Triple Sec
1 oz.	lemon juice or juice of ½ lemon

Combine ingredients in a shaker half filled with ice. Shake well. Strain into a cocktail glass.

Monkey Shine Shooter

½ oz.	bourbon liqueur
½ oz.	crème de banane
½ oz.	Irish cream liqueur

Combine ingredients in a shaker half filled with ice. Shake well. Strain into a shot glass.

SAINT PATRICK'S DAY
. . . .

There'll be the wearing of the green today and the drinking of it, too—with "Green Machine" punch, the "Shamrock," and the "Emerald Isle." Irish eyes will be smiling in song as well as in person as everyone raises a toast to St. Patrick who gives us this chance to celebrate.

Green Machine Punch

1 bottle	vodka
1 (12 oz.)	can frozen limeade concentrate
½ gallon	lemon sherbet
½ gallon	lime sherbet

Defrost limeade and dissolve in vodka. Add sherbets.

Everybody's Irish or Saint Pat

2 oz.	Irish whiskey
1 oz.	green crème de menthe
1 oz.	green Chartreuse

Pour ingredients into a mixing glass nearly filled with ice. Stir. Strain into a cocktail glass.

Emerald Isle

2 oz.	gin
1½ tsp.	green crème de menthe
3 dashes	bitters

Pour ingredients into a mixing glass nearly filled with ice. Stir. Strain into a cocktail glass.

Shamrock

1½ oz.	Irish whiskey
½ oz.	dry vermouth
½ oz.	green crème de menthe
1 tsp.	green Chartreuse

Pour ingredients into a mixing glass nearly filled with ice. Stir. Strain into a cocktail glass.

Irish Shillelagh

1½ oz.	Irish whiskey
½ oz.	light rum
½ oz.	sloe gin
1 tsp.	powdered sugar
1 oz.	lemon juice or juice of ½ lemon
¼ cup	peaches, fresh or canned, diced
¼ cup	raspberries, fresh or frozen

Combine ingredients in a blender with ice. Blend thoroughly. Pour into an old-fashioned glass. Garnish with raspberries.

Irish Coffee

2 oz.	Irish whiskey
	hot coffee
	granulated sugar to taste
	whipped cream or heavy cream

Dissolve sugar in whiskey in an Irish Coffee glass. Add coffee to within ½ inch of the brim. Top with whipped cream. An alternative is heavy cream poured carefully over the back of a spoon so that it floats on top of the coffee.

Irish Dream

½ oz.	Irish cream liqueur
½ oz.	hazelnut liqueur
½ oz.	brown crème de cacao
1 scoop	vanilla ice cream

Combine ingredients in a blender with ice. Blend thoroughly. Pour into a collins or parfait glass. Serve with a straw.

Irish Flag Shooter

1 oz.	green crème de menthe
1 oz.	Irish cream liqueur
1 oz.	Grand Marnier

Pour ingredients, in order given, into a pousse-café or cordial glass, so that they form separate layers.

FOURTH OF JULY
• • • • • • • • • • • • • • • •

Some things never change. Some things shouldn't change: parades on the Fourth of July, town fireworks, and Independence Day picnics. Everyone wants to celebrate on this birth-of-the-nation holiday, and if you're in charge of the entertainment, offer up some "Patriot Punch," recall American history with "Artillery" and "Redcoat" cocktails, and dazzle the troops with the red, white, and blue layers of "Stars and Stripes" and "Fourth of July."

Patriotic Punch

Good to look at and better to drink, this punch is wonderfully refreshing for a summer day. Adjust the alcohol and juice proportions according to the crowd, the day, and the degree of patriotic fervor.

1 liter	vodka
2 quarts	grapefruit juice
2 quarts	cranberry juice

Chill ingredients. Combine in a punch bowl with ice or an ice ring. Approximately 25 servings.

Independence Punch
(Non-alcoholic)

2 quarts	cranberry juice
1 quart	raspberry soda
1 pkg.	frozen raspberries

Chill juice and soda. Thaw raspberries. Combine in a punch bowl with ice or an ice ring. Approximately 15 servings.

American Beauty

1½ oz.	brandy
1 oz.	dry vermouth
½ tsp.	white crème de menthe
½ tsp.	grenadine
1 oz.	orange juice
1 oz.	port

Combine ingredients except port in a shaker half filled with ice. Shake well. Strain into a cocktail glass. Float the port on top.

Fourth of July

1 oz.	grenadine
1 oz.	vodka
1 oz.	blue Curaçao

Pour ingredients, in order given, into a cordial or shot glass, so that they form separate layers.

Artillery

2 oz.	gin
1/2 oz.	sweet vermouth
dash	bitters

Combine ingredients in a shaker half filled with ice. Strain into a cocktail glass.

Colonial

1 1/2 oz.	gin
1 Tbs.	Maraschino
1/2 oz.	grapefruit juice

Combine ingredients in a shaker half filled with ice. Shake well. Strain into a cocktail glass.

Stars and Stripes

3/4 oz.	cherry Herring
3/4 oz.	cream
3/4 oz.	blue Curaçao

Pour ingredients, in order given, into a cordial glass, so that they form separate layers.

Redcoat

1 1/2 oz.	light rum
1/2 oz.	vodka
1/2 oz.	apricot brandy
1/2 oz.	lime juice
1 tsp.	grenadine

Combine ingredients in a shaker half filled with ice. Strain into a cocktail glass.

HALLOWEEN
. . . .

Halloween is supposed to be for kids and it's certainly a good excuse to act like one. Have a costume party and everyone can be ridiculous together. Drinking something called the "Frisky Witch" is silly enough, but the "Witch's Tit"? Come on. Oh, sure, the devil made you do it. Maybe so. He's been drinking too many "Black Magic" shooters and his costume looks awfully real.

Halloween Cider Punch

2 quarts	hard cider
6 oz.	Drambuie
6 oz.	dry sherry
1/4 cup	sugar
2 oz.	lemon juice
2 cups	sparkling water
4	apples, sliced

Add all ingredients to a punch bowl with a block of ice. Garnish with apple slices. Makes approximately 15 servings

Harvest Punch (Non-alcoholic)

1 quart	apple cider
2 cups	orange juice
1/2 cup	grapefruit juice
1 quart	lemon and lime soda
1 quart	sparkling water
	apple and orange slices

Add juices to a punch bowl with a block of ice. Stir. Add sodas. Stir well. Garnish with fruit.

Frisky Witch

1 1/2 oz.	vodka
1/2 oz.	Sambuca

Pour into an old-fashioned glass over ice.

Witch's Tit

2 oz.	coffee liqueur
1/2 oz.	heavy cream
one half	maraschino cherry

Pour coffee into a cordial or pousse-café glass first. Add cream by pouring over the back of a spoon so that it floats on top. Place cherry at the center.

Devil's Tail

1 1/2 oz.	light rum
1 oz.	vodka
2 tsp.	apricot brandy
2 tsp.	grenadine
1/2 oz.	lime juice

Combine ingredients in a blender with ice. Blend thoroughly. Pour into a champagne flute.

Green Devil

1 1/2 oz	gin
1 oz.	crème de menthe
1/2 oz.	lime juice

Combine ingredients in a shaker half filled with ice. Shake well. Strain into an old-fashioned glass over ice.

Green Demon Shooter

½ oz.	vodka
½ oz.	rum
½ oz.	Midori
½ oz.	limeade

Combine ingredients in a shaker half filled with ice. Shake well. Strain into a shot glass.

Devil's Cocktail

2 oz.	ruby port
1 oz.	dry vermouth
splash	lemon juice

Pour ingredients into a mixing glass nearly filled with ice. Stir. Strain into a cocktail glass.

Black Magic Shooter

2 oz.	vodka
1 oz.	coffee liqueur

Combine ingredients in a shaker half filled with ice. Shake well. Strain into a shot glass.

THANKSGIVING

Giving thanks is something we all could be better at, and Thanksgiving gives us a chance to realize our good intentions, and enjoy a feast. Hot punches like Glögg and Mulled Cider fortify us for joyful overeating. "Shirley Temples" help the children feel grown up. A cocktail called the "Thanksgiving Special" should be carried to the cook, who deserves a good portion of the thanks for the day.

Thanksgiving Special

1 oz.	gin
¾ oz.	apricot-flavored brandy
¾ oz.	dry vermouth
splash	lemon juice

Combine ingredients in a shaker half filled with ice. Shake well. Strain into a cocktail glass.

Happy Apple

2 oz.	rum
3 oz.	apple cider
½ oz.	lime juice

Combine ingredients in a shaker half filled with ice. Shake well. Strain into an old-fashioned glass. Garnish with a lime twist.

Mayflower Cocktail

1½ oz.	sweet vermouth
½ oz.	dry vermouth
½ oz.	brandy
1 tsp.	Pernod
1 tsp.	Triple Sec
dash	orange bitters

Combine ingredients in a shaker half filled with ice. Shake well. Strain into a cocktail glass.

Americana

¼ oz.	Tennessee whiskey
1 tsp.	fine sugar
dash	bitters
	champagne, chilled

Combine the whiskey, sugar, and bitters in a collins or highball glass until the sugar is dissolved. Fill with champagne.

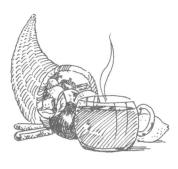

Shirley Temple
(Non-alcoholic)

	ginger ale
½ tsp.	grenadine
	maraschino cherry,
	orange slice

Pour ginger ale into an old-fashioned glass over ice. Add grenadine and stir gently. Garnish with a cherry and orange slice.

Turkey Shooter

| ¾ oz. | Wild Turkey bourbon |
| ¼ oz. | white crème de menthe |

Pour ingredients into a mixing glass nearly filled with ice. Stir. Strain into a cordial glass or a brandy snifter.

Glögg

2 bottles	dry red wine
1 Tbs.	cognac
½ cup	fine sugar
5	cloves
2 sticks	cinnamon
	raisins
	slivered almonds

Combine all ingredients except raisins and almonds in a saucepan and heat. Do not boil. Serve with almonds and raisins on the side to be added to the mug or punch cup when the drink is poured. About 10 servings.

Mulled Cider Punch (Non-alcoholic)

2 gallons	apple cider
2	lemons, sliced
2	oranges, sliced
5	cinnamon sticks
1 Tbs.	cinnamon
1 Tbs.	nutmeg
6	cloves

Combine all ingredients in a large pot. Heat just to boiling. Makes approximately 20 servings.

Tom and Jerry

2 oz.	light rum
1 oz.	brandy
2 tsp.	sugar
1	egg white
1	egg yolk
6 oz.	hot milk
	nutmeg

Beat the egg white and yolk separately. Mix them together in a mug. Add the sugar and mix vigorously. Pour in the rum and brandy. Fill with milk. Stir gently and sprinkle with nutmeg.

CHRISTMAS
. . . .

Christmas is for gathering, so a wonderful punch bowl seems ideal for the whole family. Irresistible Egg Nog is a treat with or without rum. Wassail, the traditional old English holiday drink, was originally made with ale, roasted apples, toasted bread, raisins, and currants. Too much for today's taste, but here is a marvelous modern version. The name is derived from the old Gaelic toast, *Was Hael!,* Be Well! Indeed. And merry, merry Christmas.

Egg Nog

6	eggs
1 cup	sugar
1/2 tsp.	salt
1 cup	rum
1 1/2 tsp.	vanilla
1 quart	light cream or milk
	nutmeg

Beat eggs until light and foamy. Add sugar, salt, and vanilla. Add rum and cream. Stir well. Chill. Sprinkle with nutmeg before serving. Makes approximately 12 half-cup servings.

Sparkling Orange Egg Nog (Non-alcoholic)

1 quart	orange juice, chilled
1/4 cup	lemon juice
3	eggs
2 Tbs.	sugar
dash	cinnamon
dash	cloves
1 pint	vanilla ice cream
16 oz.	ginger ale, chilled

Beat eggs until light and foamy. Add 2 cups of the orange juice, lemon juice, sugar, and spices and stir well. Chill. Just before serving add ice cream and remaining 2 cups of orange juice and beat with a hand mixer. Add ginger ale and mix briefly. Sprinkle with nutmeg.

Joy to the World

1 1/2 oz.	light rum
1/2 oz.	bourbon
1/2 oz.	dark crème de cacao

Pour ingredients into a mixing glass nearly filled with ice. Stir. Strain into a cocktail glass.

Christmas Pousse-Café

| 1 part | grenadine |
| 1 part | green crème de menthe |

Pour grenadine into a cordial glass first. Then carefully pour crème de menthe over the back of a spoon so that the layers remain.

Yuletide Punch (Non-alcoholic)

1 quart	water
1 cup	fine sugar
1 can	frozen lemonade (concentrate)
1 quart	cranberry juice
2 cups	apple juice or cider
1 cup	orange juice
2 cups	ginger ale

Heat water and sugar to boiling until sugar is dissolved. Cool. Combine all ingredients in a punch bowl over ice. Makes about 20 servings.

Wassail

¼ tsp.	nutmeg
¼ tsp.	cardamom
¼ tsp.	powdered ginger
2	cloves
2	cinnamon sticks
1 cup	water
2 bottles	medium dry sherry
½ cup	brandy
1 cup	sugar
3	egg yolks
6	egg whites
4	baked apples

Simmer the spices in a large saucepan for 10 minutes. Add liquors and sugar; heat, but do not boil. Remove from heat. Lightly beat egg yolks and whites separately (they should be no more than frothy). Pour a cup of the warm sherry into a punch bowl and stir in the egg yolks. Add the rest of the liquor. Beat in the egg whites with a whisk until foamy. Float apples. Makes approximately 12 servings.

NEW YEAR'S EVE

New Year's Eve can be terribly elegant or downright silly with crazy hats and creaky noisemakers. Why not combine the two? Let your guests decide. Let them choose the sophistication of "Bubbly Mint" in champagne flutes and "Coffee Nut," with Frangelico and Amaretto, in fine china cups. Or let them say good-bye to the old year with paper horns and "Snakebite" in a shot glass. Either way, the new year is coming!

Champagne Punch

1 bottle	dry white wine
16 oz.	grapefruit juice
1	pineapple, diced and crushed in a blender, or one large can of crushed pineapple
1 bottle	champagne, chilled

Combine all ingredients except the champagne in a punch bowl. Add ice and chilled champagne just before serving. Makes about 15 servings.

Spirited Raspberry Punch
(Non-alcoholic)

1 (12 oz.)	can frozen raspberry juice
1 (12 oz.)	can frozen lemonade
1 quart	ginger ale, chilled
1 pint	raspberry sherbet

Dilute the juices two to one with water. Before serving, add ginger ale. Spoon sherbet into punch.

Champagne Cooler

1 oz.	brandy
1/2 oz.	Triple Sec
1 tsp.	fine sugar champagne, chilled

Combine brandy, Triple Sec, and sugar in a large wine glass. Add champagne and garnish with a sprig of mint.

Bubbly Mint

1/2 oz.	white crème de menthe champagne, chilled

Pour crème de menthe into champagne glass and add champagne to fill.

Happy Youth

1 oz.	cherry brandy
2 oz.	orange juice
1 tsp.	fine sugar champagne, chilled

Dissolve sugar in brandy and orange juice in a champagne glass. Fill with champagne.

Single Egg Nog

1	egg
1 1/2 oz.	rum (or liquor of choice)
6 oz.	milk nutmeg

Combine ingredients in a shaker half filled with ice. Shake well. Strain into a highball glass without ice. Sprinkle with nutmeg.

Non Egg Nog
(Non-alcoholic)

1	egg
1/4 tsp.	almond extract
1/4 tsp.	vanilla extract
1 Tbs.	fine sugar
6 oz.	milk nutmeg

Combine ingredients in a shaker half filled with ice. Shake well. Strain into a highball glass without ice. Sprinkle with nutmeg.

Night Cap

2 oz.   light rum
1 tsp.   fine sugar
         warm milk
         nutmeg

Pour ingredients into a mug. Stir.
Sprinkle with nutmeg.

Kamikaze Shooter

½ oz.   vodka
½ oz.   Triple Sec
½ oz.   lime juice

Combine ingredients in a shaker half
filled with ice. Shake well. Strain into
a shot glass.

Coffee Nut

1 oz.   Amaretto
1 oz.   Frangelico
         hot black coffee
2 oz.   cream or whipped
         cream

Pour ingredients except cream into a
mug. Top with whipped cream or
cream poured over the back of a
spoon to float on top.

Snakebite Shooter

1½ oz.   Yukon Jack
1 oz.   lime juice or
         juice of ½ lime

Combine ingredients in a shaker half
filled with ice. Shake well. Strain into
a shot glass.

PARTYING AT THE PARTY

There's "party," the noun, as in "I'm giving a party." And there's "party," the verb, as in "I'm going to party." The trick is to do both at the same time. So here are some suggestions for entertaining evenings with unifying themes. The drinks range from break-the-ice punches to quiet-down coffees. You'll need food, of course. But, as everyone knows, the drinks make the party.

BEACH BLAST
• • • • • • • • • • • • • • • • •

No summer should go by without a beach party. Get out the bathing suits, the umbrellas, the towels, and demand sun. Make your own if you have to with "Costa del Sol." Mix up a batch of Rum Fruit Punch, post recipes for sun-struck drinks like "Laughing at the Waves," stock the bar, and sink your toes into the sand. Make yourself a "Beach Bum," and be one. What else is a party for?

Beachcomber

1½ oz.	light rum
½ oz.	Maraschino
1 tsp.	fine sugar
½ oz.	lime juice

Combine ingredients in a shaker half filled with ice. Shake well. Strain into a cocktail glass.

Bikini Beachcomber
(Non-alcoholic)

5 oz.	peach nectar
1 oz.	raspberry syrup
1 oz.	fresh lime juice

Combine ingredients in a shaker half filled with ice. Shake well. Strain into a cocktail glass.

Rum Fruit Punch

1 liter	rum
2 cups	pineapple juice
½ cup	lemon juice
1 cup	fine sugar
½ cup	water
one half	pineapple, sliced
1 pint	strawberries, sliced

In a saucepan, heat water and sugar until boiling. Cool. Combine all ingredients except fruit in a punch bowl over ice. Add fruit just before serving. Makes approximately 35 servings.

Laughing at the Waves

1½ oz.	vodka
½ oz.	dry vermouth
½ oz.	Campari

Pour ingredients into a mixing glass nearly filled with ice. Stir. Strain into a cocktail glass.

Costa del Sol

2 oz.	gin
½ oz.	apricot brandy
½ oz.	Cointreau

Combine ingredients in a shaker half filled with ice. Shake well. Strain into an old-fashioned glass.

Barbary Coast

1 oz.	gin
1/2 oz.	scotch
1/2 oz.	light rum
1/2 oz.	white crème de cacao
1 oz.	light cream

Combine ingredients in a shaker half filled with ice. Shake well. Strain into a cocktail glass.

Shark Attack

2 oz.	vodka
4 oz.	lemonade
2 dashes	grenadine

Pour ingredients into a collins or highball glass over ice. Stir well. Serve with a straw.

Beach Bum

2 oz.	light rum
1/2 oz.	Triple Sec
1/2 oz.	lime juice
dash	grenadine
	lime wedge
	granulated sugar

Sprinkle sugar on a saucer. Rub a lime wedge on the rim of a cocktail glass and dip the glass in sugar to coat the rim. Combine ingredients in a shaker half filled with ice. Shake well. Strain into the glass.

Surf's Up

½ oz.	crème de banane
½ oz.	white crème de cacao
5 oz.	pineapple juice
1 oz.	light cream

Combine ingredients in a blender with ice. Blend thoroughly. Pour into a collins or parfait glass. Garnish with a fruit slice and cherry.

Virgin Island
(Non-alcoholic)

3 oz.	pineapple juice
1 oz.	coconut cream
1 oz.	lime juice or juice of ½ lime
½ tsp.	orgeat (almond) syrup

Combine ingredients in a blender with ice. Blend thoroughly. Pour into a collins or parfait glass.

Beach Blanket Bingo
(Non-alcoholic)

4 oz.	white grape juice
3 oz.	cranberry juice
	club soda

Pour juices into a highball glass over ice. Stir. Add club soda. Stir gently. Garnish with a fruit wedge.

Caribbean Coffee

2 oz.	dark rum
1 tsp.	granulated sugar
4 oz.	hot coffee
	cream or whipped cream

Dissolve sugar in coffee in an Irish Coffee glass or mug. Add rum. Stir well. Float cream on top by pouring over the back of a spoon.

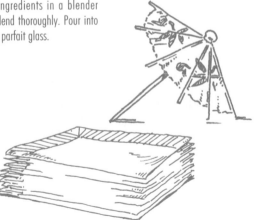

MEXICAN MAYHEM
• • • • • • • • • • • • • • • • • • •

It's easy to slip into the mood of a Mexican party. Wear a sombrero. Drink a "Sombrero." Remember Chiquita Banana? Drink a "Chiquita" with bananas. Salsa, hot green and mild red, supplies the spice. Tequila, with cola, with juice, and even with coffee, delivers the spirit.

Tequila Punch

1 liter	tequila
4 bottles	chilled sauterne
1 bottle	chilled champagne
8 cups	diced fruit
	fine sugar to taste

Pour tequila, wine, and fruit into a punch bowl. Add ice and champagne just before serving. Makes approximately 40 servings.

Cactus Bite

1½ oz.	tequila
1 oz.	lemon juice or juice of ½ lemon
2 tsp.	Cointreau
2 tsp.	Drambuie
½ tsp.	fine sugar
dash	bitters

Combine ingredients in a shaker half filled with ice. Shake well. Strain into a cocktail glass.

Sombrero

2 oz.	coffee liqueur
2 oz.	light cream

Pour liqueur into an old-fashioned glass over ice. Float cream on top.

Mexicana

2 oz.	tequila
1 oz.	pineapple juice
½ oz.	lemon juice
1 tsp.	grenadine

Combine ingredients in a shaker half filled with ice. Shake well. Strain into a cocktail glass.

Mexicola

2 oz.	tequila
	cola
	lime wedge

Pour over ice into a collins or highball glass. Squeeze and add lime wedge.

Jumping Bean

1½ oz.	tequila
½ oz.	Sambuca
3	coffee beans

Pour ingredients into a mixing glass nearly filled with ice. Stir. Strain into a cocktail glass. Add coffee beans

Chiquita

1½ oz.	vodka
½ oz.	banana liqueur
½ oz.	lime juice
¼ cup	sliced bananas
1 tsp.	orgeat (almond) syrup

Combine ingredients in a blender with ice. Blend thoroughly. Pour into a collins or parfait glass. Serve with a straw.

Frozen Matador

1½ oz.	tequila
1 oz.	pineapple juice
1 oz.	orange juice
1 Tbs.	lime juice

Combine ingredients in a blender with ice. Blend thoroughly. Pour into a collins or parfait glass. Garnish with fruit.

Tijuana Taxi

1½ oz.	gold tequila
1 oz.	blue Curaçao
1 oz.	passion fruit liqueur
4 oz.	lemon and lime soda

Pour liquors into a highball glass over ice. Stir. Add soda to fill. Garnish with fruit and a cherry.

Way to Juarez
(Non-alcoholic)

1 oz.	orange juice
2 oz.	passion fruit or tropical juice
4 oz.	lemon and lime soda

Pour juices into a highball glass over ice. Stir. Add soda to fill. Garnish with fruit.

Border Crossing

2 oz.	tequila
1 tsp.	Rose's lime juice
1 tsp.	lemon juice
4 oz.	cola

Pour ingredients into a highball glass nearly filled with ice. Stir. Garnish with a lime wedge.

Spanish Moss

1 oz.	coffee liqueur
1 oz.	tequila
1 oz.	green crème de menthe

Pour ingredients into a mixing glass nearly filled with ice. Stir. Strain into a cocktail glass.

Mexican Coffee

$\frac{1}{2}$ oz.	tequila
1 oz.	coffee liqueur
1 oz.	hot coffee
1 oz.	heavy cream

Pour coffee into an Irish Coffee glass or mug. Add tequila and liqueur. Stir well. Float the cream on top by pouring it over the back of a spoon.

DERBY DRINKS

The "Preakness," the "Belmont," the "Derby"—are there better excuses for a party, or a drink? For everyone who makes a wager, hopes to win, and feels the rush as horses head for the finish line, a gathering of friends is the place to be. Horse races generate their own excitement. All you have to do is provide the place, the spirits, a lick of good luck, and faith in a winning ticket.

Mint Julep Punch

1 cup	mint jelly
4 cups	water
$3\frac{1}{2}$ cups	bourbon
6 cups	pineapple juice
$\frac{1}{4}$ cup	lime juice
6 cups	lemon and lime soda

Heat mint jelly in saucepan with 2 cups of the water until the jelly melts. Cool. Add the rest of the ingredients except the soda. Pour into a punch bowl over a block of ice. Add soda and stir gently. Approximately 25 servings.

Winner's Circle Punch (Non-alcoholic)

6 cups	tea, chilled
2 cups	sugar
2 cups	orange juice
3 cups	pineapple juice
1/2 cup	lime juice
1 quart	ginger ale

Combine all ingredients in a punch bowl over ice. Makes approximately 25 servings.

Aqueduct

1 1/2 oz.	vodka
1 tsp.	white Curaçao
1 tsp.	apricot-flavored brandy
1 tsp.	lemon juice
1 tsp.	lime juice

Combine ingredients in a shaker half filled with ice. Shake well. Strain into a cocktail glass. Add a lemon twist.

Preakness

1 1/2 oz.	blended whiskey
1/2 oz.	Benedictine
1 tsp.	brandy
dash	bitters

Combine ingredients in a shaker half filled with ice. Shake well. Strain into a cocktail glass. Add a lemon twist.

Derby Special

1 1/2 oz.	light rum
1/2 oz.	Cointreau
1 oz.	orange juice
1/2 oz.	lime juice

Combine ingredients in a blender with ice. Blend thoroughly. Pour into a cocktail glass.

Belmont

2 oz.	gin
1/2 oz.	raspberry syrup
3/4 oz.	light cream

Combine ingredients in a shaker half filled with ice. Shake well. Strain into a cocktail glass.

Belmont's Beauty (Non-alcoholic)

3 oz.	cran-raspberry drink
1 oz.	club soda
1 scoop	vanilla ice cream

Combine ingredients in a blender without ice. Blend thoroughly. Pour into a collins or highball glass.

Turf

1½ oz.	gin
1½ oz.	dry vermouth
¼ oz.	Pernod
1 Tbs.	lemon juice
2 dashes	bitters

Combine ingredients in a shaker half filled with ice. Shake well. Strain into a cocktail glass.

Jockey Club

1½ oz.	gin
½ tsp.	white crème de cacao
splash	lemon juice

Combine ingredients in a shaker half filled with ice. Shake well. Strain into a cocktail glass.

Horse's Neck

This drink is traditionally served with a spiral cut from a whole lemon. The spiral is placed in a collins or highball glass, with one end over the rim, the "horse's neck" stretching to the finish.

2 oz.	blended whiskey
dash	bitters
	ginger ale
	lemon rind spiral

Place the lemon rind in the glass. Fill with ice. Add whiskey, bitters, and then ginger ale. Stir.

Stirrup Cup

1 oz.	brandy
1 oz.	cherry-flavored brandy
1 oz.	lemon juice or juice of ½ lemon
1 tsp.	sugar

Combine ingredients in a shaker half filled with ice. Shake well. Strain into an old-fashioned glass over ice.

SOUTHERN SOIREE
• • • • • • • • • • • • • • • • • •

Mix the gentility of southern mint and peaches with the kick of "Rebel" punch and you've got the right brew for this party. Extend a little Dixie hospitality with down-home grits and catfish, and wave everyone good-bye with a "Ya'll come back real soon, y'hear!"

Rebel Punch

1 pint	brandy
1 pint	bourbon
1 quart	club soda
1 (12 oz.)	can pineapple juice concentrate
¼ cup	fresh lemon juice
2 oz.	grenadine
2 bottles	sparkling rosé

Combine all ingredients except the wine. Stir and chill. Pour over ice into punch. Add wine just before serving. Makes about 25 servings.

Magnolia Mint Punch (Non-alcoholic)

15 sprigs	mint
1 cup	granulated sugar
1 quart	boiling water
1 cup	lemon juice
1 quart	orange juice
1 quart	pineapple juice
1 quart	ginger ale
	mint and lemon slices for garnish

Combine mint, sugar, and water in a saucepan. Simmer for 10 minutes. Refrigerate. To assemble punch, strain mint syrup and add to punch bowl with all ingredients except ginger ale. Add soda just before serving. Makes approximately 25 servings.

Kentucky Colonel

2 oz.	bourbon
1 oz.	Benedictine

Pour ingredients into a mixing glass nearly filled with ice. Stir. Strain into a cocktail glass. Add a lemon twist.

Southern Bride

1½ oz.	gin
1 tsp.	Maraschino
1 oz.	grapefruit juice

Combine ingredients in a shaker half filled with ice. Shake well. Strain into a cocktail glass.

Scarlett O'Hara

2 oz.	Southern Comfort
2 oz.	cranberry juice
1 oz.	lime juice or juice of ½ lime

Combine ingredients in a shaker half filled with ice. Shake well. Strain into a cocktail glass.

Georgia Peach

1½ oz.	vodka
1 oz.	peach-flavored brandy
1 tsp.	lemon juice
1 tsp.	peach preserves
1 wedge	canned or fresh peach, cut up

Combine ingredients in a blender with ice. Blend thoroughly. Pour into a collins or highball glass.

Darling Peaches (Non-alcoholic)

3 oz.	peach nectar
1 tsp.	lemon juice
1 Tbs.	peach preserves
1 tsp.	honey
1 wedge	canned or fresh peach, cut up

Combine ingredients in a blender with ice. Blend thoroughly. Pour into a collins or highball glass.

Magnolia Maiden

1½ oz.	bourbon
1 oz.	Grand Marnier
½ tsp.	fine sugar
splash	lemon juice
splash	club soda

Combine bourbon, Grand Marnier, sugar, and lemon juice in a shaker half filled with ice. Shake well. Strain into an old-fashioned glass with ice. Add club soda. Stir gently.

Rebel Yell

1½ oz.	bourbon
½ oz.	Cointreau
1 oz.	lemon juice or juice of ½ lemon
1	egg white

Combine ingredients in a shaker half filled with ice. Shake well. Strain into an old-fashioned glass. Garnish with an orange slice.

Dixie Whiskey

2 oz.	bourbon
1 tsp.	white crème de menthe
1 tsp.	Triple Sec
½ oz.	fine sugar
dash	biters

Combine ingredients in shaker half filled with ice. Shake well. Strain into a cocktail glass.

HAWAIIAN LUAU

When winter is at its coldest, when days are at their shortest, it's time to think Hawaiian—leis and grass skirts, rolling hips and the "Hula Hula." Have a party with drinks like the "Maui Breeze," with intimations of tropical air. And the "Polynesian Pepper Pot," that warms you up from the inside out. Add a ukulele and the "Hawaiian Love Song" and you've got all the heat you need.

Honolulu Punch

1 liter	light rum
½ cup	dark rum
½ cup	Triple Sec
¼ cup	fine sugar
½ cup	lemon juice
2 cups	orange juice
2 cups	pineapple juice

Combine all ingredients in a punch bowl over ice. Garnish with fruit. Makes approximately 15 servings.

Blue Hawaiian

1½ oz.	light rum
1 oz.	blue Curaçao
2 oz.	coconut cream
3 oz.	pineapple juice

Cobine ingredients in a blender with ice. Blend thoroughly. Pour into a collins or parfait glass. Garnish with fruit slice and cherry.

Blue Hawaiian Shake (Non-alcoholic)

½ cup	blueberries, fresh or frozen
2 oz.	coconut cream
4 oz.	milk

Combine ingredients in a blender with ice. Blend thoroughly. Pour into a collins or parfait glass. Garnish with fruit slice and cherry.

Hawaiian Cocktail

2 oz.	gin
½ oz.	Triple Sec
½ oz.	pineapple juice

Combine ingredients in a shaker half filled with ice. Shake well. Strain into a cocktail glass.

Hawaiian Lemonade (Non-alcoholic)

3 oz.	pineapple juice
4 oz.	lemonade

Combine lemonade and pineapple juice in a collins or highball glass over ice. Garnish with fruit.

Maui Breeze

½ oz.	Amaretto
½ oz.	Triple Sec
½ oz.	brandy
1 oz.	lemon juice or juice of ½ lemon
1 tsp.	fine sugar
2 oz.	pineapple juice
2 oz.	guava juice

Combine ingredients in a blender with ice. Blend thoroughly. Pour into a collins or parfait glass. Garnish with fruit and a cherry.

Polynesian Pepper Pot

1½ oz.	vodka
1 oz.	dark rum
4 oz.	pineapple juice
1/2 oz.	orgeat (almond) syrup
4 dashes	Tabasco sauce
dash	curry powder

Combine ingredients except curry powder in a shaker half filled with ice. Shake well. Strain into a highball glass. Sprinkle curry on top. Serve with a straw.

Pure Polynesian Pepper Pot (Non-alcoholic)

4 oz.	pineapple juice
½ oz.	orgeat (almond) syrup
1 oz.	lemon juice or juice of ½ lemon
4 dashes	Tabasco sauce
dash	curry powder

Combine ingredients except curry powder in a shaker half filled with ice. Shake well. Strain into a highball glass. Sprinkle curry on top. Serve with a straw.

Hula Hula

2 oz.	gin
1 oz.	pineapple juice
1 Tbs.	Cointreau
¼ tsp.	fine sugar

Combine ingredients in a shaker half filled with ice. Shake well. Strain into a cocktail glass.

Waikiki Beachcomber

1½ oz.	vodka
½ oz.	raspberry liquer
4 oz.	guava juice
1 oz.	lime juice or juice of ½ lime

Combine ingredients except liquer in a shaker half filled with ice. Shake well. Strain into a cocktail glass. Float liquer on top.

Part VII
APÉRITIFS BEFORE...
LIQUEURS AFTER

Apéritifs, Liqueurs, Pousse-Café

To Whet the Appetite: The Apéritif

If the cocktail hour is, indeed, to be a brief prelude before dinner, the perfect drink may be the apéritif. Light and flavorful, an apéritif is an anticipation, an enticement to the appetite. Apéritifs are aromatic wines treated with special flavorings such as herbs, barks, and flowers. They may also be fortified with spirits like brandy. Vermouth, both dry and sweet, is an apéritif. Quinine is added to apéritifs such as Dubonnet and Byrrh. Lillet is sweet, red or white, and Campari is rather bitter and often served with soda to make a sparkling refresher, enjoyable at any time.

Negroni

1 oz.	Campari
1 oz.	sweet vermouth
1 oz.	gin

Pour all ingredients into an old-fashioned glass over ice. Stir gently.

Dry Negroni

1 oz.	Campari
1 oz.	dry vermouth
1 oz.	gin

Pour all ingredients into an old-fashioned glass over ice. Stir gently.

Vermouth Apéritif

| 2 oz. | sweet vermouth |
| | lemon twist |

Pour over ice in an old-fashioned glass. Add a lemon twist.

Bittersweet Cocktail

1 oz.	sweet vermouth
1 oz.	dry vermouth
	lemon twist

Pour ingredients into a mixing glass nearly filled with ice. Stir. Strain into a cocktail glass. Add a lemon twist.

Vermouth Cassis

2 oz.	dry vermouth
1 oz.	cassis
	club soda

Combine vermouth and cassis in a highball glass nearly filled with ice. Pour soda. Stir gently. Garnish with a lemon twist.

Coronation

3 oz.	dry sherry
$1/2$ oz.	dry vermouth
dash	Maraschino
dash	bitters

Combine ingredients in a shaker half filled with ice. Shake well. Strain into a cocktail glass. Serve with an olive and a lemon twist.

Campari and Soda

2 oz.	Campari
	club soda or
	sparkling water
	lime wedge

Combine in a highball glass over ice. Squeeze and add a lime wedge.

Americano

1 oz.	Campari
1/2 oz.	sweet vermouth
	club soda

Combine Campari and sweet vermouth in an old-fashioned glass over ice. Stir. Top with club soda. Garnish with an orange slice.

Dubonnet Cocktail

1 oz.	Dubonnet
1 oz.	gin
	lemon twist

Pour ingredients into a mixing glass nearly filled with ice. Stir. Strain into a cocktail glass. Add a lemon twist.

Baronial

2 oz.	Lillet
1 oz.	gin
splash	Cointreau
dash	bitters

Pour ingredients into a mixing glass nearly filled with ice. Stir. Strain into a cocktail glass.

Dubonnet Rouge or Bently

| 2 oz. | Dubonnet |
| 1 oz. | apple brandy |

Pour ingredients into a mixing glass nearly filled with ice. Stir. Strain into a cocktail glass.

Macintosh Rouge (Non-alcoholic)

2 oz.	apple juice
2 oz.	grapefruit juice
1/2 tsp.	grenadine

Combine ingredients in a shaker half filled with ice. Shake well. Strain into a cocktail glass.

Armagnac Lilli

4 oz.	Lillet
1 oz.	Armagnac
	orange wedge

Pour over crushed ice in a champagne glass. Garnish with an orange wedge.

Amer Picon Cocktail

2 oz.	Amer Picon
1 oz.	lime juice or
	juice of ½ lime
1 tsp.	grenadine

Combine ingredients in a shaker half filled with ice. Shake well. Strain into a cocktail glass.

Jellybean

1½ oz.	brandy
½ oz.	anisette

Pour ingredients into a mixing glass nearly filled with ice. Stir. Strain into a cocktail glass.

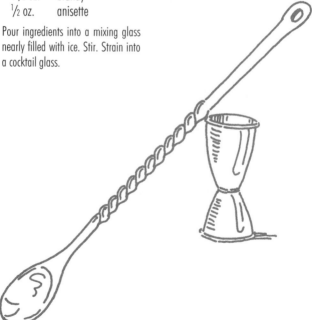

LIQUEUR: THE CORDIAL DRINK

"Liqueur" and "cordial" are synonymous designations for delectably sweet concoctions that are often served as after-dinner drinks, but are also used as ingredients in cocktails. Liqueurs have a spirit or brandy base, a syrup of sugar or honey, and a flavor derived from aromatic substances such as flowers, fruits, peels, berries, barks, herbs, seeds, roots, or spices. The unique, and often secret, combination of these ingredients is each liqueur's hallmark.

Served straight, in its own glass, a liqueur is sweetly seductive. Indeed, with a 2.5 percent minimum sugar content, liqueurs are the dessert of drinks. Many are even sweeter, and the crèmes, whose creamy consistency stems from a high sugar content, are the richest of all. But their sweetness never overwhelms their fruit or herb character, so all liqueurs will add intense, distinctive flavors to mixed drinks.

The following is a partial list of liqueurs and their predominant flavors:

Aquavit: caraway
Amaretto: almond
Anisette: anise seed (licorice)
Apricot brandy: apricot

Bailey's Irish Cream: cream
Benedictine: herbs and spices
Chambord: black raspberry
Chartreuse, yellow or green:
      herbs and spices
Cherry Heering: cherry
Cocoribe: coconut
Cointreau: orange peel
Cranberria: cranberry
Crème de Cacao, dark or white: cacao bean
Crème de Cassis: black currants
Crème de Menthe, green or white:
      peppermint leaves
Crème de Noyaux: almond
Crème Yvette: violet leaves
Curaçao, white or blue: orange and spice
Drambuie: scotch and honey
Frangelico: hazelnut
Grand Marnier: orange and cognac
Kahlúa: coffee
Kummel: caraway
Maraschino: cherry
Midori: melon
Sloe Gin: sloe berry
Southern Comfort: whiskey and peach
Tia Maria: coffee
Triple Sec: orange

Queen Elizabeth

1 oz.   Benedictine
2 oz.   sweet vermouth

Combine ingredients in a shaker half filled with ice. Shake well. Strain into a cocktail glass.

Proserpine's Revenge

1 oz.   white crème de menthe
1 oz.   cognac

Pour crème de menthe into a cocktail glass. Float cognac on the top by adding slowly. Serve with a short straw.

Cortés

1 oz.   Kahlúa
1 oz.   light rum
dash   lemon juice

Serve over cracked ice in a brandy snifter.

Hamlet

1 oz.   Peter Heering
1 oz.   Aquavit

Serve ice cold in a cordial glass.

Foreign Affair

1 oz.   Sambuca
1 oz.   brandy

Pour ingredients into a mixing glass nearly filled with ice. Stir. Strain into a cocktail glass.

Sambuca Straight

2 oz.   Sambuca
3   coffee beans

Pour into a brandy snifter and add coffee beans.

Peppermint Pattie Shooter

1½ oz.   dark crème de cacao
1½ oz.   white crème de menthe

Pour crème de cacao into a shot glass. Follow with crème de menthe.

Jellybean Shooter

½ oz.   blackberry brandy
½ oz.   anisette

Pour ingredients into a mixing glass nearly filled with ice. Stir. Strain into a shot glass.

Mocha Mint

1 oz.   coffee brandy
1 oz.   white crème de cacao
1 oz.   crème de menthe

Combine ingredients in a shaker half filled with ice. Shake well. Strain into a cocktail glass.

Creamsicle

1½ oz.   Amaretto
1½ oz.   orange juice
         milk or cream

Pour ingredients into a mixing glass nearly filled with ice. Stir. Strain into a highball glass over ice.

Melon Ball

2 oz.   Midori
1 oz.   vodka
        grapefruit juice

Pour ingredients into a mixing glass nearly filled with ice. Stir. Strain into a highball glass over ice.

B-52 Shooter

½ oz.   Grand Marnier
½ oz.   Irish cream liqueur
½ oz.   coffee liqueur

Serve in a shot glass.

Peanut Butter and Jelly Shooter

¾ oz.   Frangelico
¾ oz.   Chambord

Serve in a shot glass.

THE POUSSE-CAFÉ: RAINBOW IN A GLASS

The pousse-café is the dazzler of bartending, a chance to create something original with a touch of glamour. A pousse-café is a rainbow cordial made of different colored liqueurs poured so carefully that the layers remain separate, floating on top of each other. The separation is possible because each liqueur has a specific gravity or weight. By pouring the heaviest first, and continuing with liqueurs of decreasing weights, the layers will not mix. Carefully pour each liqueur down a bar spoon handle, over the edge of the glass into a smooth, flat layer. Use a pousse-café glass or a tall cordial glass.

Follow the weights below and create your own rainbows.

Anisette (50 proof)	17.8
Crème de Noyaux (50 proof)	17.7
Crème de Menthe (60 proof)	15.9
Crème de Banane (50 proof)	15.0
Maraschino (50 proof)	14.9
Coffee liqueur (50 proof)	14.2
Cherry liqueur (48 proof)	12.7
Parfait Amour (50 proof)	12.7
Blue Curaçao (60 proof)	11.7
Blackberry liqueur (50 proof)	11.2
Apricot liqueur (58 proof)	10.0
Orange Curaçao (60 proof)	9.8
Triple Sec (60 proof)	9.8
Coffee-flavored brandy (70 proof)	9.0
Peach-flavored brandy (70 proof)	7.0
Cherry-flavored brandy (70 proof)	6.8
Apricot-flavored brandy (70 proof)	6.6
Rock & Rye liqueur (60 proof)	6.5
Ginger-flavored brandy (70 proof)	6.4
Peppermint Schnapps (60 proof)	5.2
Kummel (78 proof)	4.2
Peach liqueur (60 proof)	4.1
Sloe gin (60 proof)	4.0

Golden Glow

1 part	green crème de menthe
1 part	Galliano
1 part	blackberry brandy

Fifth Avenue

1 part	dark crème de cacao
1 part	apricot brandy
1 part	cream

Angel's Delight

1 part	grenadine
1 part	Triple Sec
1 part	crème Yvette
1 part	cream

Café Chartreuse

1 part	grenadine
1 part	yellow Chartreuse
1 part	crème de cassis
1 part	crème de menthe
1 part	green chartreuse

PART VIII
WINE AND CHAMPAGNE

Choosing a Wine, Wine Glossary,
Vintages, Mixed Drinks with Wine,
Champagne: Served Straight or
with a Mix

WINE

Spicy, rich, mellow, light, meaty, flowery, muscular, buttery, earthy, elegant, delicate, intricate, and even austere—wine is all of these and more, a vast multifaceted, intriguing adventure in enjoyment. While wine is fascinating to devotées and intimidating to initiates, behind the bar it is a basic ingredient in some lively, interesting drinks. To mix a wine spritzer or a kir, or to offer wine at a party, requires nothing more than a down-to-earth knowledge and a reasonable approach to buying.

There are four types of wine: still, aromatized, sparkling, and fortified. Aromatized wines are described in the chapter on apéritifs and sparkling in the section on champagne in this chapter. Still, wines are the familiar red, white, and rosé that, very generally, range from dry and semi-dry, to sweet. Fortified wines are braced with a strong spirit, often brandy, and include, among others, the port wines of Portugal and the sherries of Spain.

THE BOTTLE CHASE: CHOOSING A WINE
. . . .

Facing the forest of wine bottles at the liquor store can be daunting. The list below describes wines in the most general way with the barest descriptions. Many wines that are French, German, or Italian are also produced by American vineyards. The best way to learn about wine is to investigate and experiment with the sure understanding that individual taste is the best standard for personal pleasure. White wines are served chilled and red wines are served at room temperature.

Red Wines

Cabernet Sauvignon	Full-bodied
Burgundy	Range from dry to semi-sweet
Bordeaux	Forceful
Beaujolais	Fresh, light
Pinot Noir	Dry, delicate
Merlot	Soft, fruity
Zinfandel	Robust
Petit Syirah	Full-bodied
Chianti	Dry, fruity

White Wines

Sauvignon Blanc	Herbaceous
Chenin Blanc	Medium sweet to dry
Chardonnay	Full-bodied
Chablis	Dry, white Burgundy
Sauterne	Sweet Bordeaux
Riesling	Flowery
Gewurtztraminer	Pungent

Dessert and Appetizer Wines

| Port: ruby, tawny, and vintage | Fortified with brandy. Sweet |
| Sherry | Fortified with brandy. Dry to sweet |

Sparkling Wines

| Sparkling Burgundy | Red and dry |
| Champagne | See section on champagne in this chapter |

WINE GLOSSARY: ENGLISH SPOKEN HERE

Wine words are not a foreign language but the most common vocabulary does take on new meanings when associated with wine. Ordinary definitions can sometimes be a guide. Think, for example, of a wine said to be "weak," and the meaning, quite logically, is that it has little character. More often, definitions of how a wine tastes are an attempt to go where no words can, into the sensory experience that is fully felt but ephemeral and, to a great extent, indefinable. The following is a list of words related to the creation, bottling, labeling, and tasting of wine that can be defined...almost.

Words to Know: Wine Clarification

Aging	Effects of maturation
Alcoholic fermentation	The process by which yeast and sugar in grapes react to produce alcohol, turning grape juice to wine
AC	*Appellation d'Origine Contrôlée*— Quality control designation on French wine
Claret	English term for red wine
Demi-Sec (French)	Medium sweet
Doux (French)	Sweet
Fortified wine	Wine with a high-strength spirit added
Jug wine	American term for table wine
Sec (French)	Dry
Tannin	Natural component in skins, seeds, and stems of grapes. Creates a dry, puckering sensation in the mouth.
Varietal	Grape variety. Wines made from a single grape are "varietals," and labeled with that grape.
Vintage	Defines the grape harvest of a single year
Wood aging	Aging of wine in barrels, casks, or vats of wood

The Wine Advocate's Vintage Guide 1990-1998

REGIONS	1990	1991	1992	1993	1994	1995	1996	1997	1998
St. Julien/Pauillac St. Estephe	98T	75R	79E	85T	87T	93T	94T	87E	85T
Margaux	90E	74R	75E	85T	86T	88E	88T	86E	86T
Graves	90R	74R	75E	86T	88E	89E	86E	87E	89E
Pomerol	95E	58C	82R	87T	89T	92T	85E	88R	96T
St. Emilion	98T	59C	75R	84C	86T	88E	87T	87R	96T
Barsac/Sauternes	96T	70E	70C	70C	78E	85E	87E	89E	90E
Côte de Nuits (Red)	92R	86T	72C	80C	72C	90T	92T	88R	83E
Côte de Beaune (Red)	90R	72E	70C	74C	70C	89T	92T	88R	80E
White	87R	70C	90R	72C	87R	91E	92E	89R	86R
North-Côte Rôtie	92T	92E	78E	58C	88E	90T	86T	90E	90T
South-Châteauneuf du Pape	95E	65C	78R	85T	86T	92T	82R	82R	96E
Beaujolais	86C	88C	77C	80C	85C	87C	82C	87R	84R
Alsace	93R	75R	85R	87R	90R	89R	86R	87E	90E
Loire Valley (Sweet White)	90R	75R	80R	86R	87R	88R	91E	82R	84R
Champagne	96E	N.V.	N.V.	88E	N.V.	87E	91E	86R	86C
Piedmont	96E	76E	74C	86E	77C	87C	95T	96E	96E
Tuscany	90E	85T	72C	86T	85C	88T	78R	95E	86C
Germany	92E	85E	90R	87R	90R	87R	93T	88E	85E
Vintage Port	N.V.	90E	95E	N.V.	92T	N.V.	N.V.	89T	N.V.
Rioja	87E	76E	85E	87E	90E	90E	85E	86R	82C
Penedes	87E	74E	82E	87E	90E	89E	82E	86R	78C
New So. Wales & Victoria	88E	89E	87R	87R	90E	87E	90E	88R	95E
Cabernet Sauvignon	94E	94T	93E	93T	95E	94T	90T	94E	85T
Chardonnay	90C	85C	92C	90C	88R	92R	87R	92R	87R
Zinfandel	91R	91R	90R	90R	92R	87R	89E	85E	86C
Pinot Noir	86R	86R	88R	88R	92R	88R	88R	90E	87R
Pinot Noir	90C	87C	88R	89R	92R	76C	86C	87C	92E
Cabernet Sauvignon	87R	85C	89E	87E	90E	86E	88T	88T	90C

Side labels: BORDEAUX, BURGUNDY, RHÔNE, ITALY, SPAIN, AUST, CALIFORNIA COAST, ORE/WASH

KEY (General Vintage Chart)

- 90-100 = The Finest
- 80-89 = Above Average to Excellent
- 70-79 = Average
- 60-69 = Below Average
- Below 60 = Appalling

EXPLANATION OF SYMBOLS

- C = Caution, too old or irregular in quality
- E = Early maturing and accessible
- T = Still Tannic or Youthful
- R = Ready to drink
- NV = Non-Vintage

Used with permission from Robert M. Parker, Jr.'s. The Wine Advocate, P.O. Box 311, Monkton, MD 21111 © Copyright 2000

For subscription information, call 410-329-6477 or fax us at 410-357-4501

Taste Test: Words on the Tip of the Tongue

Acid/Acidity	Crisp, lively quality
Aromatic	Wines with pronounced aroma, especially spicy
Balance	Harmony among components: acidity, tannins, fruit, and alcohol
Clean	With no defects in aroma, appearance, or flavor
Complex	Multifaceted aroma and flavor. For a wine to be considered great, it must be complex.
Delicate	Light fragrance, body, and flavor
Fruity	Aroma of grapes or other fruits
Fullness	The feel and weight of wine in the mouth
Green	Unripe or tart
Oaky	Slight vanilla flavor from aging in oak casks
Velvety	Smooth and rich in texture

MIXED DRINKS WITH WINE

There is no substitute for a wine that you truly enjoy, but there is a place for wine as an ingredient in a mixed drink. Combine wine with the bubble of sparkling water for a refreshment with less overall alcohol content. Try the flavor enhancement of a liqueur or fruit juice for a change of pace. These are light-hearted drinks with unpretentious ingredients and flexible proportions. That's what makes them so appealing.

Sangria

1 bottle	dry red wine
2 oz.	Triple Sec
1 oz.	brandy
2 oz.	orange juice
1 oz.	lemon juice or juice of ½ lemon
¼ cup	fine sugar
10 oz.	club soda, chilled orange and lemon slices

Chill all ingredients together except club soda for at least one hour. Before serving, pour into a pitcher or punch bowl over ice and add club soda. Makes approximately 10 servings.

Red or White Wine Spritzer

| 4 oz. | wine |
| 2 oz. | club soda or sparkling water wedge of lemon or lime |

Pour wine over ice into a large wine glass. Add club soda. Stir gently. Garnish with a fruit wedge.

White or Red Wine Cooler

| 4 oz. | wine |
| 2 oz. | pineapple juice club soda or sparkling water wedge of lemon or lime |

Pour wine, juice, and soda over ice into a large wine glass. Stir gently. Garnish with a fruit wedge.

Pineapple Sparkler (Non-alcoholic)

| 4 oz. | pineapple juice |
| 1 tsp. | fine sugar club soda or sparkling water wedge of lemon or lime |

Combine juice and sugar in a shaker half filled with ice. Shake well. Strain into a wine glass. Add soda. Garnish with fruit.

Kir

| ½ oz. | crème de cassis (or to taste) |
| 4 oz. | dry white wine |

Pour the cassis into a large wine glass. Add the wine. Do not stir. The cassis is meant to be at the bottom so the drink gets sweeter as it diminishes. More white wine can then be added if desired. Serve with a lemon twist.

Carefree Kir (Non-alcoholic)

| 1 oz. | raspberry syrup |
| 4 oz. | white grape juice |

Pour syrup into a wine glass over ice. Add grape juice. Stir. Serve with a lemon twist.

Bishop

4 oz.	red wine
2 oz.	orange juice
1 oz.	lemon juice or juice of ½ lemon
1 tsp.	fine sugar

Pour juices and sugar into a mixing glass nearly filled with ice. Stir. Strain into a highball glass over ice. Fill with red wine. Garnish with a fruit slice.

Valentine

4 oz.	Beaujolais
1 tsp.	cranberry liqueur
2 oz.	cranberry juice

Combine ingredients in a shaker half filled with ice. Shake well. Strain into a wine glass.

A Touch of the Bubbly: Champagne

Champagne is sexy, no doubt about it. Its bubbles are flirtatious, its fizz is an invitation to hold hands, to sigh and exchange glances. "Champagne" is a term often used to describe any sparkling wine, but that is wrong. Genuine champagne is only produced in France, in the Champagne region: chalky hills and valleys near the River Marne. But the champagne method (*méthode champenoise*) of fermenting wine in the bottle it is sold in can be used anywhere to make still wine sparkle. Here's how it's done.

The method begins with a *cuvée*, a vineyard's blend of dry white wines. The blend is bottled with yeast and sugar for a second fermentation to create the bubbles. In the process a sediment is formed. *Mon Dieu!* No matter how fine the wine, gunk in the bottle will not do. So the second step ingeniously collects the sediment. The bottles are tilted and turned so that the sediment clings to the cork. In the third step, the cork (along with the unsightly muck) is removed, a bit of sugar is added, and the bottle is recorked. The typical mushroom-shaped cork is a result of ramming two-thirds of a cork wider than the neck into the bottle. Under pressure, the cork forms a perfect seal. The wire on top is to prevent any over-exuberant bubbles from popping their cork.

A champagne bottle should be opened with the same caution used in handling a dangerous weapon. Imagine the bottle as a gun and your finger as the safety catch. Always keep a thumb or finger over the cork. First remove the foil and wire, with your thumb hovering over the cork. Then point the bottle at a 45-degree angle away from everybody. Grip the cork firmly in one hand and pull with the other. Never turn the cork. As the internal pressure loosens the cork, continue to hold it firmly.

Champagne offers choices but also clear descriptions. Created in a range from dry to sweet, the contents of the bottles are conveniently labeled. *Brut* is very dry; "Extra Dry" or *Sec* is not as dry; *Demi-Sec* is the half-and-half of champagne, slightly sweet and dry; and *Doux* is the sweetest of all.

Not Really Champagne Punch (Non-alcoholic)

1 cup   fine sugar
1 cup   water
2 cups   grapefruit juice
          juice of 1 lemon
1½ quarts ginger ale (36 oz.)

Dissolve sugar in water. Add grapefruit and lemon juices. Add ginger ale to punch bowl just before serving. Makes approximately 20 servings.

Champagne Cocktail

1 tsp.   fine sugar
3 dashes bitters
6 oz.   champagne, chilled

Dissolve sugar in bitters in the bottom of a champagne flute. Add champagne. Stir. Top with a lemon twist.

Mimosa

3 oz.   chilled champagne
3 oz.   orange juice

Combine in a champagne flute or white wine glass. Stir gently.

Midori Mimosa

2 oz.   Midori
1 tsp.   Rose's lime juice
4 oz.   champagne, chilled

Combine in a champagne flute or white wine glass. Stir gently.

Mimi's Mimosa (Non-alcoholic)

3 oz.   sparkling white
          grape juice, chilled
3 oz.   orange juice

Pour orange juice into a champagne glass until half full. Add grape juice. Stir gently.

Bellini

2 oz.	peach nectar
1/2 oz.	lemon juice
	chilled champagne.

Pour juices into a champagne flute. Stir. Fill with champagne. Stir gently.

Baby Bellini (Non-alcoholic)

2 oz.	peach nectar
1 oz.	lemon juice or juice of 1/2 lemon sparkling cider, chilled

Pour peach nectar and lemon juice into a champagne flute. Add sparkling cider to fill. Stir gently.

Champagne Mint

1/2 oz.	green crème de menthe chilled champagne to fill

Pour crème de menthe into a champagne flute. Add champagne. Stir gently.

Champagne Charisma

2 oz.	champagne, chilled
1 oz.	Vodka
1/2 oz.	peach-flavored brandy
1 oz.	cranberry juice
1-2 scoops raspberry sherbet	

Combine all ingredients except champagne in a blender. Blend well. Pour into a large red wine goblet. Add champagne. Stir.

Champagne Fizz or Diamond Fizz

2 oz.	gin
1 oz.	lemon juice or juice of 1/2 lemon
1 tsp.	sugar
4 oz.	champagne

Combine gin, lemon juice, and sugar in a shaker half filled with ice. Shake well. Strain into a highball glass over ice. Add champagne. Stir gently.

Buck's Fizz

5 oz.	champagne, chilled
1/2 oz.	Triple Sec
1 oz.	orange juice
1/2 tsp.	grenadine

Pour champagne, Triple Sec, and orange juice into a champagne flute. Add grenadine. Stir. Garnish with an orange slice.

Scotch Royale

1 1/2 oz.	scotch
1 tsp.	fine sugar
dash	bitters
	chilled champagne
	to fill

Dissolve sugar in bitters and scotch in a champagne flute. Fill with champagne. Stir gently.

Kir Royale

1 oz.	crème de cassis
	chilled champagne
	to fill

Pour ingredients into a champagne flute or wine glass. Stir gently.

Faux Kir Royale (Non-alcoholic)

1 oz.	raspberry syrup
	chilled sparkling
	white grape juice

Use a wine glass. Pour syrup over ice. Add juice. Stir well and garnish with a lemon twist.

PART IX
BEER—THE BEST OF THE BREW

Varieties, Microbreweries, Beer Clubs,
Home Brewing, Mixed Drinks with Beer

MAKE MINE A BEER

To think of beer as a generic and rather plebeian drink is pure beverage snobbery. Man has been brewing beer for thousands of years, since the moment he remained in one place long enough to grow grain. The variations have been increasing ever since. There are probably over 20,000 styles of beer in the world, and some people would like to try them all. The differences are in the yeast, the hops, and the fermentation. The distinctions can be subtle and elegant or blunt and rough. Beers can be light or heavy, sweet or astringently dry; there are ales or lagers, but they all have character. Here are a few personalities:

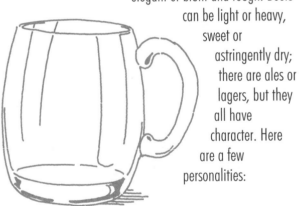

ALES

• •

Bitter, a light ale whose name reflects its taste.

Mild, a brown ale, light-bodied and thirst quenching.

Pale, a light-colored, tangy brew.

Brown, a dark ale, sweeter than pale.

Stout, a black ale characterized by the sharpness of roasted barley.

Porter, a dark ale whose flavor comes from dark malts.

LAGERS

• •

Lagers, brought from Germany, are the most prevalent and popular in the United States.

Pilsener, a name that refers to the style that originated in Pilzen, Czechoslovakia. Most American lagers are light Pilseners.

Boch, a dark, strong, malty lager.

MICRO TO THE MAX: MICROBREWERIES ARE BURGEONING

It is the paradox of the high-tech era that hand-crafted products are becoming increasingly desirable. Enter the crafted beer. Microbreweries, which make their own beers, and brewpubs, which make and serve them, are sprouting up all over the country, finding a niche the giant companies are too big to squeeze into. The Institute for Brewing Studies reported explosive growth in this industry. And that growth is based on smallness. The comparison of these beers to the corporate kind is to liken a hunk of rich textured, whole grain, home-baked bread to a slice of supermarket white. Words like tangy, full-bodied, robust, and flowery have real meaning in this context. There are microbreweries in most states now. If there isn't one nearby, move.

*Denotes brewery with on-site restaurant or pub.

Alabama
Microbreweries

Birmingham Brewing Co.*
Birmingham, Alabama

Alaska
Microbreweries

Alaskan Brewing and Bottling Co.*
Juneau, Alaska

Bird Creek Brewery
Bird Creek, Alaska

Raven Ridge Brewing Co.*
Fairbanks, Alaska

Arizona
Microbreweries

Black Mountain Brewing Co.*
Cave Creek, Arizona

California, Northern
Regional Breweries

Sierra Nevada Brewing Co.*
Chico, California

Microbreweries

American River Brewing Co.
Auburn, California

Anderson Valley Brewing Co.*
Boonville, California

Etna Brewing Co.*
Etna, California

Hangtown Brewery
Placerville, California

Humbolt Brewery and Micro
Arcata, California

Humes Brewing Co.
Glen Ellen, California

Mad River Brewing Co.
Blue Lake, California

Mendocino Brewing Co.*
Hopland, California

Moonlight Brewing Co.
Santa Rosa, California

Murphy's Creek Brewing Co.
Murphy's, California

Napa Valley Ale Works*
Napa, California

Nevada City Brewing Co.
Nevada City, California

North Coast Brewing Co.*
Fort Bragg, California

Pacific Hop Exchange
Novato, California

Tuscan Brewing Co.
Red Bluff, California

California, Bay Area
Regional Breweries

Anchor Brewing Co.*

Microbreweries

Bay Brewing Co.
Devil Mountain Brewery
Benicia, California

Golden Pacific Brewing Co.*
Emeryville, California

Lind Brewing Co
San Leandro, California

California, Central
Microbreweries

Covany Brewing Co.
Grover Beach, California

El Toro Brewing Co.*
 Morgan Hill, California

San Andreas Brewing Co.
 Hollister, California

St. Stans Brewery, Pub and Restaurant
 Modesto, California

California, Southern Microbreweries
 Angeles Brewing Co.
 Chatsworth, California

Heritage Brewing Co.
 Lake Elsinore, California

Old Columbia Brewery
 Associated Microbrewers
 San Diego, California

Old River Brew Co.*
 Bakersfield, California

Southern California Brewing Co.
 Torrance, California

Colorado
Regional Breweries

Rockies Brewing Co.*
 Boulder, Colorado

Microbreweries

Avery Brewing Co.*
 Boulder, Colorado

H. C. Berger Brewing Co.*
 Fort Collins, Colorado

Breckenridge Brewery and Pub*
 Breckenridge, Colorado

Breckenridge Brewery, Denver*
 Denver, Colorado

Bristol Brewing Co.*
 Colorado Springs, Colorado

Broadway Brewing Co.
 Denver, Colorado

Coophouse Brewery
 Broomfield, Colorado

Durango Brewing Co.
 Durango, Colorado

Golden City Brewery
 Golden, Colorado

Great Divide Brewing Co.*
 Denver, Colorado

Irons Brewing Co.*
 Lakewood, Colorado

Left Hand Brewing Co.*
 Longmont, Colorado

Lone Wolfe Brewing Co.
 Carbondale, Colorado

Lonetree Brewing Ltd.
 Denver, Colorado

Namaqua Brewing Co.*
 Loveland, Colorado

New Belgium Brewing Co.*
 Fort Collins, Colorado

Odell Brewing Co.*
 Fort Collins, Colorado

Pikes Peak Brewery
 Colorado Springs, Colorado

Silver Plume Brewing Co.
 Silver Plume, Colorado

Snowy Mountain Brewing Co.
 Grand Junction, Colorado

Connecticut
Microbreweries

New England Brewing Co.*
 Norwalk, Connecticut

New Haven Brewing Co.*
New Haven, Connecticut

Florida
Regional Breweries

The Florida Brewery Inc.*
Auburndale, Florida

Microbreweries

Beach Brewing Co.
Orlando, Florida

Ybor City Brewing Co.
Tampa, Florida

Georgia
Microbreweries

The Atlanta Brewing Co.
Atlanta, Georgia

Marthasville Brewing Co.
Atlanta, Georgia

Hawaii
Microbreweries

Ali'i Brewing Co.
Honolulu, Hawaii

Kona Brewing Co.
Kealakekua, Hawaii

Idaho
Microbreweries

The Beier Brewing Co.
Boise, Idaho

Coeur D'Alene Brewing Co.
T. W. Fisher's "A Brewpub"*
Coeur D'Alene, Idaho

McCall Brewery Co.
McCall, Idaho

Sun Valley Brewing Co.*
Hailey, Idaho

Thunder Mountain Brewery
Ketchum, Idaho

Illinois
Microbreweries

Chicago Brewing Co.*
Chicago, Illinois

Golden Prairie Brewing Co.
Chicago, Illinois

Pavichevich Brewing Co.
Elmhurst, Illinois

Star Union Brewing Co.*
Hennepin, Illinois

Indiana
Regional Breweries

Evansville Brewing Co.*
Evansville, Indiana

Microbreweries

Indianapolis Brewing Co.*
Indianapolis, Indiana

Mishawaka Brewing Co.*
Mishawaka, Indiana

Oaken Barrel Brewing Co.
Greenwood, Indiana

Iowa
Regional Breweries

Brandevor USA/Dubuque Brewing and
Bottling Co.*
Dubuque, Iowa

Microbreweries

Dallas County Brewing Co.
Old Depot Restaurant*
Adel, Iowa

Millstream Brewing Co.*
Amana, Iowa

Kansas
Microbreweries

Miracle Brewing Co.
Wichita, Kansas

Kentucky
Microbreweries

Oldenberg Brewery/Drawbridge Inn*
Fort Mitchell, Kentucky

Louisiana
Regional Breweries

Abita Brewing Co.*
Abita Springs, Louisiana

Dixie Brewing Co. Inc.
New Orleans, Louisiana

Microbreweries

Rikenjaks Brewery
Jackson, Louisiana

Maine
Microbreweries

Andrew's Brewing Co.*
Lincolnville, Maine

Atlantic Brewing Co.*
Bar Harbor, Maine

Bar Harbor Brewing
Bar Harbor, Maine

Casco Bay Brewing Co.
Portland, Maine

D. L. Geary Brewing Co. Inc.*
Portland, Maine

Lake St. George Brewing Co.
Liberty, Maine

Shipyard Brewery
Portland, Maine

Maryland
Microbreweries

Frederick Brewing Co.*
Frederick, Maryland

Oxford Brewing Co.*
Linthicum, Maryland

Wild Goose Brewery*
Cambridge, Maryland

Massachusetts
Microbreweries

Atlantic Coast Brewing Co.*
Boston, Massachusetts

The Berkshire Brewing Co. Inc.
South Deerfield, Massachusetts

Boston Beer Co.*
Boston, Massachusetts

Essex Brewing Co. Ltd.
Bradford, Massachusetts

Ipswich Brewing Co.

Old Harbor Brewing Co.*
Ipswich, Massachusetts

Lowell Brewing Co.*
Lowell, Massachusetts

Mass. Bay Brewing Co.
Boston, Massachusetts

Middlesex Brewing Co.
Burlington, Massachusetts

Olde Salem Village Brewing Co.
Danvers, Massachusetts

Old Newbury Brewing Co.
Newbury, Massachusetts

Michigan
Microbreweries

Duster's Microbrewery Co.
Lawton, Michigan

Frankenmuth Brewery
Frankenmuth, Michigan

Kalamazoo Brewing Co. Inc.
Kalamazoo, Michigan

Minnesota
Regional Breweries

Cold Spring Brewing Co.
Cold Spring, Minnesota

Minnesota Brewing Co.
St. Paul, Minnesota

Pete's Brewing Co.
St. Paul, Minnesota

August Schell Brewing Co.
New Ulm, Minnesota

Microbreweries

James Page Brewing Co.*
Minneapolis, Minnesota

Summit Brewing Co.*
St. Paul, Minnesota

Missouri
Microbreweries

Boulevard Brewing Co.*
Kansas City, Missouri

Montana
Microbreweries

Bayern Brewing Inc./Iron Horse Pub*
Missoula, Montana

Bridger Brewing Co.*
Belgrade, Montana

Himmelberger Brewing Co.
Billings, Montana

Kessler Brewing Co.*
Helena, Montana

Lang Creek Brewery*
Marion, Montana

Milestown Brewing Co.*
Miles City, Montana

Montana Brewing Co.*
Billings, Montana

Rock'n Brewing*
Belgrade, Montana

Spanish Peaks Brewing Co.*
Bozeman, Montana

Whitefish Brewing Co.
Whitefish, Montana

New Hampshire
Microbreweries

Smuttynose Brewing Co.
Portsmouth, New Hampshire

New Mexico
Microbreweries

Russell Brewing Co.
Santa Fe, New Mexico

Santa Fe Brewing Co.
Galisteo, New Mexico

New York
Regional Breweries

F. X. Matt Brewing
Utica, New York

Microbreweries

Buffalo Brewing Co.*
Buffalo, New York

Lake Titus Brewery*
Malone, New York

Woodstock Brewing Co.*
Kingston, New York

North Carolina

Microbreweries

Dilworth Microbrewery*
Charlotte, North Carolina

Gate City Brewing Co.*
Greensboro, North Carolina

Smokey Mountain Brewery
Waynesville, North Carolina

Weeping Radish Brewery (No. 2)
Durham, North Carolina

Wilmington Brewing Co. Inc.*
Wilmington, North Carolina

Ohio

Regional Breweries

Hudepohl-Schoenling Brewing Co.
Cincinnati, Ohio

Microbreweries

Columbus Brewing Co.
Columbus, Ohio

Crooked River Brewing Co.*
Cleveland, Ohio

Lift Bridge Brewing Co.
Ashtabula, Ohio

Oregon

Regional Breweries

Full Sail Brewing Co.*
Hood River, Oregon

Bridge Port Brewing Co.
Portland, Oregon

Portland Brewing Co. (No. 2)
Portland, Oregon

Widmer Brewing Co.*
Portland, Oregon

Microbreweries

Bandon Brewing Co./Bandon-by-the-
Sea*
Bandon, Oregon

Deschutes Brewery (No. 2)
Bend, Oregon

Deschutes Brewery and Public House*
Bend, Oregon

Edgefield Brewery
Troutdale, Oregon

Full Sail Brewing Co. (No. 2)/
The Pilsener Room*
Portland, Oregon

Hair of the Dog Brewing Co.
Portland, Oregon

Mt. Hood Brewing Co.*
Government Camp, Oregon

Multnomah Brewery
Portland, Oregon

Oregon Trader Brewing Co.
Albany, Oregon

Oregon Trail Brewery
Corvallis, Oregon

Portland Brewing Co.
Portland, Oregon

Rogue Ales Brewery/Oregon Brewing Co.*
Newport, Oregon

Saxer Brewing Co.*
Lake Oswego, Oregon

Star Brewing Co.
  Portland, Oregon

Willamette Valley Brewing Co./Nor'
  Wester Pub*
  Portland, Oregon

Pennsylvania
Regional Breweries

Jones Brewing Co.
  Smithton, Pennsylvania

Latrobe Brewing Co.*
  Latrobe, Pennsylvania

The Lion Inc.*
  Wilkes-Barre, Pennsylvania

Straub Brewery
  St. Mary's, Pennsylvania

D. G. Yuengling and Son Inc.
  Pottsville, Pennsylvania

Microbreweries

Arrowhead Brewing Co.
  Chambersburg, Pennsylvania

Pennsylvania Brewing Co.*
  Pittsburgh, Pennsylvania

Stoudt Brewery*
  Adamstown, Pennsylvania

White Tail Brewing Co.*
  York, Pennsylvania

South Carolina
Microbreweries

Palmetto Brewing Co.*
  Charleston, South Carolina

Tennessee
Microbreweries

Bohannon Brewing Co./Market Street
  Brewery and Public House*
  Nashville, Tennessee

Texas
Regional Breweries

Spoetzl Brewery Inc.
  Shiner, Texas

Microbreweries

Celis Brewery Inc.*
  Austin, Texas

Frio Brewing Co.*
  San Antonio, Texas

Hill Country Brewing Co.*
  Austin, Texas

Saint Arnold Brewing Co.
  Houston, Texas

Texas Brewing Co.*
  Dallas, Texas

Yellow Rose Brewing Co.*
  San Antonio, Texas

Utah
Microbreweries

Schirf Brewing Co./Wasatch Brewpub*
  Park City, Utah

Uinta Brewing Co.
  Salt Lake City, Utah

Vermont
Microbreweries

Catamount Brewing Co.*
  White River Junction, Vermont

The Magic Hat Brewing Co.*
  Burlington, Vermont

The Mountain Brewers Inc.*
  Bridgewater, Vermont

Otter Creek Brewing Inc.*
  Middlebury, Vermont

Virginia
Microbreweries

Old Dominion Brewing Co.*
  Ashburn, Virginia

Potomac River Brewing Co.*
  Chantilly, Virginia

Washington
Regional Breweries

Hart Brewing Co./Pyramid Ales*
  Kalama, Washington

Redhook Ale Brewery*
  Seattle, Washington

Redhook Ale Brewery
  Woodinville, Washington

Microbreweries

Diamond Knot Brewery
  Mukilteo, Washington

Fish Brewing Co.*
  Olympia, Washington

Hale's Ales Ltd.
  Kirkland, Washington

Hale's Ales Ltd.
  Spokane, Washington

Kelly Creek Brewing Co.
  Bonney Lake, Washington

Thomas Kemper Brewing Co.*
  Poulsbo, Washington

Mac and Jack Brewery Inc.
  Redmond, Washington

Maritime Pacific Brewing*
  Seattle, Washington

Northern Lights Brewing Co.
  Airway Heights, Washington

Onalaska Brewing Co.
  Onalaska, Washington

Pike Place Brewery*
  Seattle, Washington

Roslyn Brewing Co.
  Roslyn, Washington

Seattle Brewers
  Seattle, Washington

Whidbey Island Brewing Co.*
  Langley, Washington

Yakima Brewing and Malting Co.*
  Yakima, Washington

West Virginia
Microbreweries

Cardinal Brewing Co.*

Charleston, West Virginia

Wisconsin
Regional Breweries

Joseph Huber Brewing Co.
  Monroe, Wisconsin

Jacob Leinenkugel Brewing Co.
  Chippewa Falls, Wisconsin

Stevens Point Brewery Co.
  Stevens Point, Wisconsin

Microbreweries

Capital Brewing Co.
  Middleton, Wisconsin

Gray Brewing Co.*
  Janesville, Wisconsin

Lakefront Brewery Inc.*
  Milwaukee, Wisconsin

New Glarus Brewing Co.
  New Glarus, Wisconsin

Sprecher Brewing Co.*
  Milwaukee, Wisconsin

Wyoming
Microbreweries

Otto Brothers' Brewing Co.*
  Jackson, Wyoming

Canadian Breweries

Alberta
Regional Breweries

Big Rock Brewery Ltd.
  Calgary, Alberta

Drummond Brewing Co.
  Red Deer, Alberta

British Columbia
Regional Breweries

Okanagan Spring Brewery
  Vernon, British Columbia

Pacific Western Brewing Co.
  Prince George, British Columbia

Microbreweries

Bowen Island Brewing Co.
  Bowen Island, British Columbia

Granville Island Brewing Co.
  Vancouver, British Columbia

Horseshoe Bay Brewing Co. Ltd.
  Horseshoe Bay, British Columbia

The Nelson Brewing Co. Ltd.
  Vancouver, British Columbia

Tall Ship Ale Co.
  Squamish, British Columbia

Vancouver Island Brewing Co.
  Victoria, British Columbia

Whistler Brewing Co.*
  Whistler, British Columbia

Manitoba
Microbreweries

Fort Garry Brewing Co.
  Winnipeg, Manitoba

Northwest Territories
Microbreweries

Arctic Brewing Co.*
  Yellowknife, Northwest Territories

Ontario
Regional Breweries

The Algonquin Brewery
  Formosa, Ontario

Brick Brewing Co. Ltd.*
  Waterloo, Ontario

Lakeport Brewing Corp.
  Hamilton, Ontario

Northern Breweries Ltd.
  Sault Ste. Marie, Ontario

Sleeman Brewing and Malting Co.
  Guelph, Ontario

The Upper Canada Brewing Co.
  Toronto, Ontario

Microbreweries

Canada's Finest Beers Ltd.
  Wheatley, Ontario

The Conners Brewing Co.
St. Catharines, Ontario

Creemore Springs Brewery Ltd.
Creemore, Ontario

The Glatt Bros. Brewing Co.
London, Ontario

Great Lakes Brewing Co.
Etobicoke, Ontario

Hart Breweries Ltd.*
Carleton Place, Ontario

Hometown Breweries Ltd.
London, Ontario

Niagara Falls Brewing Co.*
Niagara Falls, Ontario

The Old Credit Brewing Co.
Port Credit, Ontario

Thames Valley Brewing Co.
London, Ontario

Trafalgar Brewing Co.
Oakville, Ontario

Wellington County Brewery Ltd.*
Guelph, Ontario

Quebec
Microbreweries

Brasal-Brasserie Allemande
Lasalle, Quebec

Brasserie McAuslan*
Montreal, Quebec

La Brasserie Portneuvoise
St. Casimir, Quebec

Les Brasseurs Du Nord Inc.*
Blainville, Quebec

Les Brasseurs G.M.T.
Montreal, Quebec

Unibroue Inc.
Chambly, Quebec

Saskatchewan
Regional Breweries

Great Western Brewing Co.
Saskatoon, Saskatchewan

BEER CLUBS DELIVER

There is an alternative way to quench a thirst for crafted beers when a home brew, U-brew, or microbrew is not available—the beer club. These are a more spirited version of the fruit-of-the-month clubs, a beer a month. Tap (pardon the pun) into their 800 numbers and, like the pizza man, they deliver. Call to discuss their microbrew labels and terms. It's easy, and so is drinking up one month's supply before the next arrives.

The following is a sampling of Beer of the Month Clubs at the time of publication:

The Brewer's Gourmet
1-800-591-BREW
42 Pope Road, Box 6611
Holliston, MA 01746

BrewTap
1-800-940-BREW
336 6th Street
San Francisco, CA 94103

Brew to You, Ltd.
1-800-800-BREW
Woodstock, IL 60098

Red, White & Brew
1-800-670-BREW
Herndon, VA 22070

HOME BREWING: WHO BREWS? YOU DO!

It's Saturday night. Time to go out, kick back, and have a brew. Or better yet, make one. The U-brew is a do-it-yourself brewery where customers make, bottle, and label their own beers. One step away from the creativity and agony of brewing at home, the U-brews offer equipment, ingredients, and guidance in a very nice social setting. U-brews even smell good. With the sweet scent of yeast and grains in the air, customers handle hops, vats, and ladles, measuring, pouring and stirring. And then they wait. Two weeks later eager amateur beer masters return for their products. Because the beer is made without preservatives, it must be drunk in six weeks, a hardship most are willing to endure.

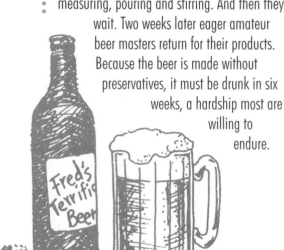

A few U-brews percolating at the time of publication:

America U-Brew
Spring Garden and Front Streets
Philadelphia, PA 19123

The Beer Store—You Brew It
637 South Broadway, Unit U
Boulder, CO 80303

Brew City
2198 Filbert Street
San Francisco, CA 94123

Custom Brew Haus
6701 Clayton Road
Clayton, MO 63117

Glisan Street Brewhaus
1402 Northwest Glisan Street
Portland, OR 97209

Hamilton Gregg Brewworks
58 11th Street
Hermosa Beach, CA 90254

MIXED DRINKS WITH BEER

People who are devoted to their beer might find it hard to imagine that a brew can team up with anything but pretzels and potato chips. But in fact, beer is a fine partner in a select few mixed drinks. Beer can be braced with whiskey, vodka, or gin and enhanced with schnapps of any flavor. And then there's the "Black Velvet," a blend of down-home stout and upscale champagne, a cultural phenomenon.

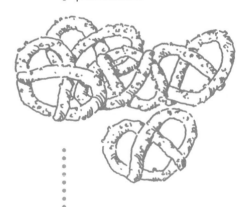

Black Velvet

| 6 oz. | stout or dark porter |
| 6 oz. | champagne or sparkling wine |

Ingredients should be chilled. Pour both into a highball glass at the same time. Do not stir.

Shandy Gaff

| 6 oz. | beer |
| 6 oz. | ginger ale |

Ingredients should be chilled. Pour both into a highball glass at the same time. Do not stir.

Black and Tan (Non-alcoholic)

| 6 oz. | ginger ale |
| 6 oz. | ginger beer |

Ingredients should be chilled. Pour both into a highball glass at the same time. Do not stir.

Depth Charge

| 2 oz. | peppermint (or any flavor) schnapps |
| 1 pint | beer |

Pour the schnapps into a frosted mug first. Top off with beer. Stir slightly.

Boilermaker

Emily Post would sip this drink after pouring the shot into the beer (pinky finger raised). Other people might drop the shot, glass and all, into the filled beer mug and chug-a-lug before the foam hits the floor.

| 1½ oz. | whiskey |
| ½ pint | beer |

Skip and Go Naked

| 1 oz. | gin |
| 1 oz. | lime juice or juice of ½ lime beer to fill |

Pour gin and juice into a chilled beer mug over ice. Fill with beer. Stir slightly.

Sneaky Pete

| 1½ oz. | apple brandy |
| ½ pint | beer |

Pour beer into a chilled mug and add applejack. Stir slightly.

Beer Buster

| 2 oz. | vodka, chilled |
| ½ pint | beer |

Pour beer into a chilled mug and add vodka. Stir slightly.

PART X
THE PARTY'S OVER

Hangovers, Responsible Drinking

THE HANGOVER: TOO MUCH OF A GOOD THING

You're having dinner out and the waiter keeps re-filling your wine glass. You're at a party and the host insists on refreshing your drink ... again. Who's counting? Your stomach, your head, and those tiny red blood cells that rush alcohol to the rest of your body. They're ringing the hangover bell, but you aren't listening. Unfortunately, you hear it in the morning when it's clanging right between your eyes.

Too much alcohol causes a hangover, but no one knows exactly why. Everyone has their own personal barometer; the quantity that brings on the symptoms is personal (age, weight, and sex count) and so are the circumstances. One prevailing theory is that dehydration is the culprit because, as the body processes liquor, it uses up a great deal of water. Another hypothesis describes a hangover as a minor withdrawal episode from an addictive substance. How minor are a great thirst, a nauseous stomach, a pounding head, and an allover feeling of anxiety? That may depend on whether you can wrap yourself around your favorite pillow and go back to sleep. A nap is as good a remedy as any.

If wakefulness is required, you will probably have to face the fact that there is no cure, only helpful possibilities. Drinking lots of water helps, and starting before bed is even better. A nonaspirin pain killer may be good for your head and kinder to your stomach than aspirin. Anyone that mentions pickles or bacon fat is talking about remedies that are peculiar to them, or just plain peculiar.

The idea of having an alcoholic drink in the morning does make some scientific sense. If several hours after drinking, your body is feeling the effects of withdrawal, a drink may help. This is the "taking a hair of the dog that bit you" theory. A Bloody Mary, page 105, or a Screwdriver, page 85, are traditional morning pick-me-ups. If coffee is more appealing, try bracing your espresso with grappa. If your mother always made you drink milk in the morning, calm yourself with a Scotch Milk Punch.

Scotch Milk Punch

2 oz.   scotch
6 oz.   milk
        fine sugar to taste
        nutmeg

Pour scotch into a highball glass. Add milk and sugar to taste. Add ice, or not, according to preference. Stir well. Dust with nutmeg. Mother knows best!

RESPONSIBLE DRINKING: MORE DOES NOT MAKE IT BETTER

The thirst-quenching embrace of a beer on a hot day, the mellowness of a good port after dinner, the crispness of an astringent cocktail, the lushness of a fruit-filled punch—these are near-perfect sensory experiences. Link them with good friends, lovers, and favorite places and they capture life's truly satisfying moments. Alcohol enhances our lives.

But alcohol is a drug, pure and simple, and it is foolish not to be aware of its dangers. It affects our bodies and brains, our judgment, coordination, and perception. The amount of alcohol that brings on these impairments is entirely individual, depending on size and weight, metabolism and age, even on the variables of a single day. And it doesn't matter what you drink: a cocktail, a beer, a five-ounce glass of wine and a three-ounce glass of sherry all have about .6 ounces of pure alcohol in them. An overdose can be fatal.

The greater tragedy is that most fatalities are not confined to the drinker. Drunk drivers are involved in nearly half of all American traffic fatalities and the innocent are often the victims. Over 20,000 people are killed in the United

States each year because of drunk driving-related accidents. Awareness and responsibility are the only factors that will make a difference.

And law enforcement. The laws vary from state to state, but police are working hard to get drunk drivers off the road. Their primary weapon is the Breathalyzer, which can count your BAC, blood alcohol content, or the percentage of alcohol in your blood. A BAC percentage as low as .05 has been found to increase the normal risk of accident by two to three times. So while you may not feel that your reflexes or judgment are impaired, if you are drinking you should not be driving. Period.

In most states a .10 BAC is considered evidence of driving under the influence of alcohol (DWI). In some states, the level is .08. The penalties range from a suspension of your driver's license for as little as a few days up to a year. Convictions include fines ranging from $100 to $500 and brief imprisonment—for the first offense. Punishment increases with repeated offenses. The BAC and the penalties are changing all the time, so check the laws of your state.

"Responsible drinking" is not an oxymoron. Moderation is the key to most pleasures. It is our responsibility as hosts, friends, and even citizens to keep people from driving drunk. In many states, it is our *legal* responsibility to do so.

To drink in moderation is not to have less fun, but to savor the drink we do have. We raise our glasses for so many joyous and solemn occasions—to the bride and groom, to the job well done, to the friend we have lost, and to the pure pleasure of the drink itself.

More does not make it better.

INDEX